Let's Talk Relationships

Second edition

Activities for Exploring Love, Sex, Friendship and Family with Young People

Vanessa Rogers

Jessica Kingsley *Publishers*
London and Philadelphia

First published in 2001 by the National Youth Agency
Second edition published in 2011
by Jessica Kingsley Publishers
116 Pentonville Road
London N1 9JB, UK
and
400 Market Street, Suite 400
Philadelphia, PA 19106, USA
www.jkp.com

Library of Congress Cataloging in Publication Data
Rogers, Vanessa.
  Let's talk relationships : activities for exploring love, sex, friendship and family with young people / Vanessa Rogers. -- 2nd ed.
     p. cm.
  ISBN 978-1-84905-136-1 (alk. paper)
  1. Interpersonal relations in adolescence. 2. Social interaction in adolescence. 3. Teenagers--Family relationships. 4. Adolescent psychology. I. Title.
  BF724.3.I58R64 2010
  158.2071'2--dc22
                              2010011058

British Library Cataloguing in Publication Data
A CIP catalogue record for this book is available from the British Library

ISBN 978 1 84905 136 1

Printed and bound in Great Britain by
MPG Books Group

Contents

Acknowledgements

I would like to thank

Zoey Caldwell, Ann McKay, Ingrid Davies, Ben Carr and Lorraine Clark (Young Citizens Project, North), Charlotte Rogers, Jeanette Williams (Young Citizens Project, South), Annie Twigg (Hertfordshire Careers Service Ltd), Deborah Morgan (Youth Offending Team, North Herts), Gillian Porter (QE11), Tony Hunt (HCC Learning Services), Catherine Ward (Dunstable Youth Offending Team), Martin Cooke, Mary Westgate and Carol Hawkes (HCC Youth Service), David Moses, Deborah Mulroney (HCC Education Department), Jani Noakes (HCC Education Welfare Services), Mike Smith (HCC Education Development Officer) and Jonathan Jack (Youth Connexions Hertfordshire).

Thanks also to any other youth workers or personal advisers not specifically named who have contributed ideas or been a part of the projects mentioned.

About the author

Vanessa is a qualified teacher and youth worker with a master's degree in Community Education. She has over ten years' experience within the Hertfordshire Youth Service both at practitioner and management levels. Prior to achieving national recognition for her work Vanessa managed a wide range of services for Hertfordshire County Council. She devises and delivers professional development training programmes, and writes for *Youth Work Now*. In addition she has been commissioned to devise training packs for a wide range of organisations, including the BBC.

This book is one of 19 resources written by Vanessa, to support the development of creative youth work and social education.

Her website www.vanessarogers.co.uk gives detailed information about further titles, training and consultancy visits.

Introduction

Encouraging young people to talk about sensitive issues and open up about their emotional hopes, fears and dreams for successful relationships with their family, boyfriend or girlfriend, peer group, those in authority or others in the wider community places a huge responsibility on those working with young people to 'get it right'.

This book creates opportunities for parents, teachers and youth workers to explore with young people what a positive relationship might be and help build the self-esteem necessary to make healthy choices.

Getting to know each other

To create a supportive environment in which young people are going to feel comfortable talking about personal things it is important to spend time getting to know each other. 'Warm ups' or 'icebreakers' are an excellent way to start work with young people. The ideas in this section offer short activities that introduce the main topic for the session and take between ten and twenty minutes. Creative, competitive or just plain fun, they provide young people with an opportunity to relax and start to get to know each other and the group facilitator.

Friendships and peer groups

Peer relationships and friendships are very important to young people. This chapter contains activities and worksheets that explore the impact and value of these. It encourages young people to look at what they can offer a prospective friend, as well as what they want, and considers the issues of trust, honesty and reciprocity.

The sessions support young people to consider things that contribute to both positive and negative friendships, including bullying. This involves exploring peer pressure and taking risks, encouraging assertiveness and equipping young people with the ability to say 'no' to unhealthy choices.

Living at home

Living at home, with parents or carers, is rarely a 100 per cent trouble-free experience for young people or the adults involved! Challenges to authority, the questioning of house rules and additional rights and responsibilities can put a strain on the most harmonious of households.

The ideas in this chapter can be used to effectively open up discussions around living at home and preparing for independent living with young people. It also includes opportunities to build negotiating skills, consider sources of conflict and develop strategies for resolving them.

Love, sex and all that

Good sex and relationships education creates opportunities for young people to reflect on positive relationships and discuss ways of communicating what they really want, as well as offering accurate information on contraception. This should be respectful of all relationships and include building skills to exercise the right to say 'no' or 'I am not ready.'

Evaluation and endings

Successful closing activities encourage young people to celebrate their achievements and help identify further learning needs. These ideas help obtain valuable feedback from young people to help inform the planning process for future work and close the session on a positive note.

Chapter 1

The Group

Before you start, consider the reasons you are setting up the group; the answer to this will determine your target group. For group work that aims to look at personal issues, such as relationships, a smaller group of about eight young people works well. You can decide if the group is to be mixed gender, but in my experience young men and women often prefer to talk about love, sex and friendship in single-sex groups. The issues that you decide to cover will also need to be age appropriate and take into account individual learning styles and cultural needs.

Environment

Try to create a relaxing environment in which to hold the sessions. Set the room up in advance using comfy chairs and soft lighting away from other users of the building and avoid interruptions during group time. Circles work well as everyone can see each other and encourage conversation.

Boundaries

Make sure that you are straight with the young people from the first session. Ensure that both you and they are aware of the boundaries that you have set for the group and also your legal duty regarding any child protection concerns. One way of explaining this to the young people is to state that the relationship they have with you and the group is confidential, unless they disclose to you that they are either at risk of being harmed or of harming someone else. Make sure that they know that you will then have a duty to act upon the information they give. The young people then have a choice of how much they wish to share.

Ground rules

Before starting, it is a good idea to produce a 'contract' or set of ground rules that everyone, including you, is happy to work with. As the issues you are hoping to explore with the group can be extremely sensitive make sure that confidentiality and the need to respect each other's points of view and experiences are fully considered. One rule that I always put forward for inclusion is that no one should ask or be asked personal questions. This enables young people to relax safe in the knowledge that embarrassing questions will not be fired at them.

Respect

It is important that the group becomes a place that nurtures and celebrates difference. Young people should be encouraged and supported in respecting differences within the group, such as sexuality, gender, disability or race. The group needs to accept that each of them will bring their own experiences of love, family, friendship and sexual relationships and that no single viewpoint is necessarily right or representative of everyone's opinion.

Participation

Encourage all members of the group to take part. It is often easier for quieter members to opt out of sessions rather than challenge the authority of more assertive young people. This can result in a few strong characters dominating the whole group and working through their own issues without thought to anyone else. With your intervention everyone should have the opportunity to speak, but also reserve the right to 'pass' if someone finds a topic really difficult to talk about.

Evaluation

The process by which you plan to evaluate the success of the group will need to be decided at the planning stage. When you agree your aims for each session, your evaluation methods should show whether these were met or missed completely! Make sure that you involve the young people in the evaluation process so that they can assess their own learning and experiences as well as providing excellent feedback for you.

Chapter 2

Getting to Know Each Other

2.1 Names

Aim

This is a quick and simple icebreaker that encourages young people to look at the possible links between their names and their cultural or family history.

You will need

- nothing!

How to do it

Ask the young people to form a circle. Place yourself and your co-worker within the group at a distance to each other.

Explain that you would like each member of the group to say their name, and then tell you a bit about the history of that name. This could be the reason they were called it, whether they like/dislike it or if they use a nickname instead.

If everybody looks a bit blank at this stage introduce yourself and demonstrate what you are asking the group to do. For example you could say something really simple like 'My name is Elizabeth and I was named after my grandmother,' or you may wish to share something more elaborate such as 'My name is Elizabeth because my mother really idolises the Queen – my brothers are called Charles and Andrew!' Finally, you could use the opportunity to introduce a nickname: 'My name is Elizabeth, but I hate it – only my mother calls me it! Everyone else calls me Beth.'

Most young people can think of something to share with the group and this is a safe way to tell a little without giving too much away!

2.2 Welcome to my world

Aim

This collage is a good way to share information about likes and dislikes, hopes and dreams and creates a visual representation of each member of the group.

You will need

- a plain stretched canvas for each person
- a good selection of magazines
- scissors
- PVA glue
- gems, sequins, glitter (optional).

How to do it

It is a good idea to make a collage of your own in advance to demonstrate. Start the session by showing this, explaining that it is representative of all the things that are important to you. Point out some of the meanings behind the images, explaining that the collage tells other people about who you are. I usually cut out letters to spell 'Welcome to my World' across mine.

Then, hand out magazines and scissors and invite the young people to look through them, cutting out things that they like doing or aspire to. Dreams and ambitions as well as things that remind them of family and friends are all welcome. Photos can be added too.

Next, give a blank canvas to each person with some PVA glue. Explain that the task is to cover the canvas with images overlapping and merging.

Facilitate a group sharing time. Each young person can show their collage to introduce themselves and explain their choices.

Display the collages to remind each other until the group knows each other better.

2.3 Introduction circle

This form of introduction works well with all ages, but for the best effect you need plenty of space to sit down and spread out a bit.

Aim

This is an icebreaker to introduce the young people to each other and the facilitator(s).

You will need

- a ball of brightly coloured string or wool.

How to do it

Make a large circle. If there is more than one facilitator, position them apart within the group.

Keeping a hold of one end, the person holding the string should throw it to another member of the group offering a welcome and introducing themselves. For example: 'Welcome to the group, my name is Krishna.' The second person to receive the string would reply, 'Welcome Krishna, my name is Hattie' and throw it to the next member. This continues until each person has been welcomed and introduced. Set a rule that each person in the group must be included to avoid anyone being left out.

As the exercise progresses you will begin to see a web forming. This is a visualisation of the process. Ask the young people to look at and reflect on the web they have made.

Finally, ask the young people to put the string down in front of them onto the ground and step away; what they can see is the interaction of the group.

2.4 My desert island

You can use this method of 'mapping' with young people of any age or gender and it works just as well in a group or individually. As it uses pictures it is ideal to use with young people who find writing difficult.

Aim

The aim of this activity is to gain an understanding of the important people in the life of each young person.

You will need

- flipchart paper

- marker pens

- stickers, glitter, string, etc. (optional).

How to do it

Explain to the group that you are giving them a once in a lifetime opportunity to create their own personal desert island. Go on to say that they can take anyone they like to the island, including friends, family and even pets!

Hand out the paper and art equipment. Make sure you point out that this not a drawing lesson; it does not matter if they use pictures, words or a mixture of both.

Allow about 15 minutes for the group to make their selections, draw their island and start to place people where they want them. Be sensitive to who is represented on the island and how young people approach the task. Next ask them to show where they would like to be on the island.

Finally, tell them they can put anyone they don't want on their island into the sea! You can enlarge upon this by introducing sharks into the water or boats to bring those they like to see occasionally to visit the island. Once everyone has finished ask the group if they would like to share their island with the other young people. If there is reluctance to share in the large group you could do this part in pairs. Are their similar choices for who is chosen? Who stays and who is in the sea? Who do they want to be with?

2.5 Hangman

This uses a game that most young people have played at some time as an icebreaker. You can use it with any size group, although with large groups you are unlikely to have the time for all the young people to have a turn.

Aim

To encourage young people to introduce something about themselves that they think identifies them.

You will need

- flipchart paper and pens.

How to do it

Decide what theme you are going to set for the game of 'hangman'. This could be a word or short phrase to outline a physical description, a like or dislike, ambition or personal achievement. It could be a 'like' such as 'dancing', or an achievement such as 'hockey captain' or a physical attribute such as 'dreadlocks' or 'pierced nose' that the young person thinks others associate with them. Make sure that the entire group is clear about what you are asking before you start.

Ask for a volunteer to go first. If there are any young people who do not know how to play, ask one of the others to explain.

The volunteer then puts the appropriate dots and dashes in place of letters to represent words on a large sheet of flipchart paper.

The rest of the group in turn calls out letters, for example 'a'. If it is in the word the volunteer writes it in. If not the volunteer should write it down at the side of the sheet. Up to ten wrong guesses are allowed before the group has run out of time and the volunteer shares their puzzle. A guess can be made at any time, but if it is incorrect the person who guessed is 'out' and cannot make any further attempts for that turn.

The person who solves the puzzle correctly goes next and sets their own task for the group to solve.

2.6 Personality plates

Aim

This is a fun way of encouraging a new group to share things about themselves by producing a collage plate that depicts each member's personality.

You will need

- large paper plates
- glue
- scissors
- marker pens
- newspaper
- magazines
- varnish.

How to do it

Make sure you have a good range of magazines and pictures before the young people arrive – there is nothing worse than discovering the only pictures you have to offer them for their collage are better suited to people over 65!

Suggest that the young people work in groups of four and hand out scissors, glue, magazines and paper plates.

Explain to the group that the idea is for each person to produce a plate that represents their personality. Offer a few examples, e.g. a picture of their favourite team if they like football, or pictures that show how they feel today.

Once everyone has finished invite the young people to display their plates, sharing the bits they feel comfortable with to introduce themselves to the group.

Finally, when the glue has dried varnish the plates to seal the pictures and use them to decorate the group area.

2.7 Clapping game

This introduction works best with large groups of young people who do not know each other well. You can make it harder by speeding up the pace as you go around the group.

Aim

The aim of the game is to go around the circle introducing the group to each other and the facilitators.

You will need

- nothing!

How to do it

Ask the young people to make a large circle, standing about arm-length apart, and then sit down.

Start off the game yourself by clapping twice and saying your name. Each young person then does the same with their own name. Place your co-worker somewhere in the second half of the circle so that they can help maintain the rhythm.

Once the circle is completed, start again. This time slapping twice on your knees, clap hands twice and motion to yourself, say your name and then motion to the person on your left and introduce them. Continue around the group so that everyone introduces themselves and someone else.

If anyone makes a mistake they are 'out' and need to put their legs out in front of them into the circle. The group carries on until only the person who remembers the most names is left.

You can repeat this again at the next group meeting to see how many names have been remembered!

2.8 Chain reaction

Aim

This warm-up exercise encourages young people to share the things they are good at and appreciate the talents of other members of the group.

You will need

- packets of paper chains
- marker pens.

How to do it

Begin by asking young people, 'What do you think that you do well?' Stress that this doesn't have to be an academic achievement but can be anything. After a brief discussion, conclude that everyone is talented in some way.

Now, hand out five of the unmade paper chains to each member of the group. Using markers, ask everyone to write one talent on each strip of paper.

Demonstrate how to create a paper chain with their strips linking their five talents together. As the young people begin to complete their mini chains, use extra strips of paper to link the mini chains together to create one long group chain. Invite the young people to stand and hold the ever-growing chain as you link it together, until everyone is linked.

Once the entire chain is constructed and linked together, hang the chain up in the room as a reminder that everyone is good at something. Encourage the young people to look at the different talents and skills within the group and refer to these during future group sessions.

2.9 Feelings

This is most effective with small groups of young people who already know each other and feel comfortable discussing emotions.

Aim

To explore feelings and how they affect the way people behave.

You will need

- copies of the 'feelings sheet'
- pens.

How to do it

Ask the young people to choose a partner. If there is an uneven number in the group work in threes. Hand out pens and a copy of the feelings sheet to each member of the group.

Explain that during this exercise individuals are free to choose how much they want to share and have the right to withhold things they do not want to discuss. This gives everyone the opportunity to be as selective as they want.

Ask the young people to look at the sheet on their own to begin with and to put a tick next to ten words that express how they feel when they feel good and a cross next to ten words that describe feeling bad.

When everyone has had time to think about the task and select words, invite them to share sheets with their partners. Spend time comparing and discussing what has been written. Are they similar? Expand upon what situations these feelings might be associated with. Ask the young people to discuss how they handle different situations, for example shyness or excitement. Close the activity by asking the group to each choose one word from the sheet that describes how they feel now.

FEELINGS SHEET

These words best describe my feelings

Angry	Embarrassed	Shy	Free
Responsible	Unsupported	Confident	Secure
Happy	Talkative	Worried	Bored
Loved	Humiliated	Innocent	Frightened
Ambitious	Trusting	Stressed	Affectionate
Unwanted	Guilty	Independent	Trusted
Attractive	Desired	Friendly	Bullied
Unfit	Healthy	Jealous	Lonely
Wanted	Blamed	Appreciated	Valued
Furious	Unloved	Hurt	Relaxed
Strong	Depressed	Energetic	Aggressive
Left out	Brave	Competitive	Unsure
Envious	Greedy	Excited	Disgusted

2.10 The pressures today

This activity works with groups of up to six young people of any age. You do need to be sensitive to gender and personal space boundaries when you agree who volunteers to be drawn around and who is doing the drawing.

Aim

This activity encourages young people to identify pressures on young people and the sources of stress.

You will need

- a very large sheet of paper
- assortment of marker pens.

How to do it

Lay the sheet out on the floor in the middle of the group. Ask one of the young people to volunteer to lie flat on the paper and be drawn around by another member of the group. This part will need to be facilitated carefully.

Once they have finished ask the young person to stand up. You should now have a life-size silhouette to work with.

Ask the young people to discuss the issues that they think lots of young people experience during their teenage years. They can then write each issue onto the silhouette with arrows going to the parts of the body they think it affects most. For example, they may agree that lots of teenagers worry about the size and shape of different parts of their body and draw arrows to these, but also to the head as the worry can affect mental and emotional health too. You should find that lots of the concerns raised result in arrows pointing to the head because of the stress they cause.

Encourage the group to think about all aspects of a young person's life and discuss each point as it is raised. Is it a universal problem? Is it a problem that is specifically age related? Are there choices or solutions that other members of the group can suggest? Who would they talk to if this was their problem? Discuss support networks and the role of friends.

2.11 Advertising me

Aim

This session aims to increase self-esteem and celebrate positive personality traits.

You will need

- magazines
- scissors
- glue
- A3 paper (approx 11 x 17")
- markers.

How to do it

Introduce the session by asking young people to consider the purpose of advertising. Talk about the methods used to get the message across – visually and with words. Explain that adverts promote the positive aspects of a product to persuade the public to buy the product.

The task for each person is to come up with an advertisement persuading someone to be their friend. The advert should depict positive aspects of themselves through pictures, words, or a combination of the two. Hand out markers, glue, scissors and magazines plus a sheet of paper each.

If anyone has a difficult time thinking of reasons someone would want to be their friend, suggest things like loyalty, trust and sense of humour. Reinforce how important these qualities are in any relationship.

At the end of the session take turns to share advertisements, encouraging members of the group to confirm the positive qualities of the presenter.

2.12 At what age can you?

This quiz is a good introduction to work around young people's rights. It should promote discussion and highlight areas of concern that you may like to explore further.

Aim

To test out young people's knowledge around the law and how it affects them. (If you are outside of the UK, please refer to the laws of your own country/state.)

You will need

- pens
- copies of the 'what age? quiz sheet' (without the answers!).

How to do it

Hand out pens and a copy of the 'what age? quiz sheet'. Explain that the questions have been taken from the *Young Citizen's Passport*, which is a compilation book of young people's rights and a guide to the law.[1]

Ask the young people to work individually on the quiz and to make a guess at anything they do not know the exact answer to. Allow around 15 minutes, depending on the size of the group.

Form a circle or gather the group together so you can talk without shouting the answers. Ask for volunteers to suggest answers and take time to discuss any points raised or answer any questions.

Once the quiz is complete ask the group to count up their scores. How aware are they of young people's rights? Are there any surprises? Which question did most get wrong?

---

1   The Citizenship Foundation (2007) *Young Citizen's Passport.* London: Hodder Education.

'WHAT AGE?' QUIZ SHEET

1.	Have your fingerprints taken by the police	10+
2.	Give consent or refuse medical or dental treatment	16
3.	Get a tattoo	18
4.	Adopt a child	21
5.	Leave home (without your parent's consent)	18
6.	Buy fireworks	18
7.	Ride a moped (up to 50cc)	16
8.	Buy a pet	12
9.	Change your name (with parental consent)	16
10.	Consent to sex	16
11.	Gamble on slot machines	Any age
12.	Buy lottery tickets or scratch cards	16
13.	Be prosecuted for not wearing a passenger seatbelt in a car	14+
14.	Become a Member of Parliament	18 (cut from 21 in 2006)
15.	Become a glamour model	18

Source: Young Citizen's Passport (updated 2007)

2.13 Reflective listening

Aim

To focus the group on a discussion which will enable them to get to know each other quickly. If the young people are already friends then it should highlight things that they don't know about each other. It introduces the concept of reflective listening and encourages the young people to listen carefully to what is being said, rather than cutting in with their own opinions.

You will need

- nothing!

How to do it

Depending on the number of young people you have in the group ask them to work in threes or fours. If it is a really small group it does work in pairs. Discuss confidentiality at this stage and reach an agreement that what is shared in the group stays there. This should encourage the participants to feel safe about talking personally.

Specify a topic to discuss within the group: 'What people usually think about me when they first meet me is…' You can demonstrate this by giving an example to start them off: 'What people think about me when they first meet me is that I have a good sense of humour!' If you think that the group might be nervous choose something less personal like 'One thing I really hate/ like is…'

Set a ground rule that only one group member can talk at a time and that the others should listen and think about what is being said.

Once each person has had their say, have a discussion within the groups. Ask the young people to reflect on any first impressions or assumptions made about each other and how these compared to what people actually said. Finally ask each person, 'Does your self-image correspond to what others think of you?'

2.14 Colours

Aim

This activity encourages young people to discuss their feelings and emotions. It can be used with groups of any age, but is most effective with no more than eight.

You will need

- pens

- squares of card in assorted colours.

How to do it

Begin the session by introducing the idea that colours can represent feelings and emotions. Make sure that you stress that this is not an exact science! Different colours may mean different things to different people. A good example of this is the colour red, which can mean anger and hate to one person and love and passion to another. Once the group has grasped the idea ask them to form smaller groups or work in pairs.

Hand out a good selection of coloured squares with a pen to each pair. Ask the young people to look carefully at the squares and think about what feelings or emotions they associate with the colours. Then, use a pen to write the word on the colour. If a colour evokes a different response from each partner, write both words on the card.

When everybody has finished ask the whole group to form a circle and discuss their findings. Is there any pattern or theme emerging? Are there many cards with two or more words on? What colours would the group choose to decorate a room to relax in? To dance in? To work in?

Finally, ask each young person to choose a colour to represent how they feel to close the session.

2.15 Newspaper game

This is a simple team game that invites young people to work together to achieve a common task. It is a versatile icebreaker as you can change the subject to suit the project you are working on.

Aim

To work in small groups to complete the challenge set as quickly as possible.

You will need

- a copy of a newspaper for each group

- scissors

- glue

- flipchart paper

- pens.

How to do it

You will need to prepare for the game by finding a newspaper that contains articles about young people. This is not usually very difficult! Remember you need a copy for each group so it needs to be current.

When the young people arrive, divide them into groups of four and hand out a copy of the newspaper, scissors, glue and a sheet of flipchart paper to each group.

Then explain that the aim of the game is to complete a series of tasks as quickly as possible by working as a team. Write the tasks up one at a time onto flipchart paper and stick them up to be referred to as the game progresses. Example tasks:

- Find an article that depicts young people in a positive way.

- Find a negative article about young people.

- Find an advert aimed at the youth market.

- Find positive images of young people with disabilities.

- Find stereotypical articles/pictures of young men.

- Find positive role models for young women.

Once they have found the articles each group then makes them into a collage on the flipchart sheet. Pens can be used to add words or put headings.

The group that completes the tasks first sticks their sheet up next to the task flipchart sheet and the game ends. A volunteer then shares with the other groups what they found and explains the collage.

Review the process with the group. What was easier to find, negative or positive images?

2.16 Famous pairs

To make this work properly you need to be able to rely on the group to follow the rules and not cheat! The more young people you have, the longer and more difficult the game is. It works well with any age or gender.

Aim

This is an icebreaker to encourage a new group to begin to talk to each other and start to interact.

You will need

*   Post-it notes with the names of famous 'pairs' on.

How to do it

Use Post-it notes to write the names of famous pairs on in advance of the session you have planned. Make sure you take some spare ones in case you get more for your group than you anticipate! For example, use cartoon couples such as Tom and Jerry, and Homer and Marge Simpson or celebrity couples, such as David and Victoria Beckham.

Once all of the young people have arrived, stick a name on each person's back. Make sure that they can't see what their own new identity is!

Now, ask the group to try and find their 'pair'. To do this they have to go around the room asking questions about the name on their own back. The catch is that they can only ask questions that can be answered 'yes', 'no' or 'don't know'! For example they can ask 'Am I male?', but not 'Am I a man or woman?' This is quite hard at first but the group should get the hang of it fairly quickly.

Once participants have discovered whose name they have on their back the next task is to find and join up with their pair. As the young people find their partner ask them to go sit down and review the process together.

At the end of the game everyone will have had the opportunity to talk with all the members of the group.

2.17 I like people who...

This icebreaker works best with groups of eight and more, with both young people and facilitators taking part.

Aim

This is a game to open up dialogue between young people and the adult or adults working with them. It is fast and fun and is a good way to get to know groups that you have not worked with before.

You will need

- chairs.

How to do it

Set up a large circle of chairs spaced fairly well apart, with one fewer chair than the total number of people participating.

Ask the young people to each find a chair and sit down. An adult then stands in the middle of the circle – they are the only person without a chair to begin the game!

The person in the middle then calls out, 'I like people who...' This has to be something true for them as well as potentially true for other members of the group. The idea is to discover commonalities, not to be as individual as possible. All those that agree with the statement must leave their chair and run around the outside of the circle as fast as they can and find another to sit on. The person who does not get a chair in time then goes into the middle and the process starts again.

IDEAS:

- support Arsenal
- watch MTV
- eat chocolate
- don't eat meat.

The game ends when the young people are exhausted!

2.18 Attitude scale

Aim

This icebreaker encourages young people to think about how they see themselves and consider how this compares with how others perceive them.

You will need

- nothing!

How to do it

Explain to the young people that the aim of this activity is to develop an attitude scale, to show the personalities within the group ranging from 'assertive' to 'passive'. The scale should form a straight line and include everyone.

Decide which end of your scale is 'assertive' and which end is 'passive' and make sure that the young people are clear about this.

Allow five to ten minutes (depending on the size of the group) for the young people to decide where they think they should stand on the scale. Position yourself on the scale too. When everybody is comfortable with his or her position on the scale, stop.

Ask the young people to look around them and reflect on what they see. Are there any surprises? Does how they see themselves fit in with other people's perception of them? What about the adult(s) running the icebreaker? Discuss the positive and negative points of both ends of the scale.

2.19 About me questionnaire

This is really a simple way to introduce young people to each other at the start of a group work programme, and is easily adapted for individual work.

Aim

This activity shares information within the group and discovers differences, similarities and common interests.

You will need

- copies of the 'about me questionnaire'
- plenty of pens.

How to do it

Ask one of the young people to hand out a sheet and pen to each member of the group.

Explain that what you want is a personal response – there is no right or wrong answer to the questions. You may want to point out that the information will be shared at the end with the group so that young people can choose what they wish to share.

Give the group about ten minutes to answer the questions, less if it is a really small group.

Each person then hands their sheet to the person on their left to read. This may be the point at which to remind the group of any contract or agreement they have about respecting each other's views and confidentiality. In turn each person then introduces the person whose card they hold.

Finally, facilitate a group discussion pulling out commonalities within the group, for example: What makes most people angry? What is the most unusual achievement?

ABOUT ME QUESTIONNAIRE

1. Something that makes me smile is . . . .

    . . . .

2. Something that really makes me angry is . . . .

    . . . .

3. If I could be anyone I would like to be . . . .

    because . . . .

4. Something that I have achieved that others may not know is . . . .

    . . . .

5. In ten years' time what I would like to be doing is . . . .

    . . . .

6. What I need to do to achieve it is . . . .

    . . . .

Chapter 3

Friendship and Peer Groups

3.1 Friendship line

This is a good way to look at friendships past and present and the importance of them to our own 'history'. It works well with small groups of young men or women.

Aim

To encourage each young person to create a friendship line which charts important people and their influences on their life.

You will need

- sheets of flipchart paper
- marker pens.

How to do it

Hand each member of the group a sheet of flipchart paper and place a good selection of markers close by.

Explain to the young people that they are going to make a 'friendship line' to depict people whose friendship has been important to them from their earliest memories to the present. This can be done using words or pictures. Next to each name ask the group to show why that person was/is important to them.

Whilst explaining the task, stress that it is up to each person to choose how much they wish to put onto paper and share. Also point out that it does not matter how many or few people are recorded on the line – this is an exercise to look at friendships and what they mean, not a competition to see who knows the most people!

Once everyone has finished, ask the group to come together and talk through the parts of their friendship line they feel comfortable sharing. Are there similarities? Have people kept in touch with their early friends? Are some friendships associated with different activities, for example sports?

3.2 Chain argument

This activity comes with a warning! Although it offers young people a forum to experience controlled arguments and compliments in equal measure you need to be very careful at setting and maintaining boundaries so that it does not become an opportunity for destructive comments and bullying.

Aim

To encourage the young people to reflect on the process that leads to conflict and also that which produces compliments. The idea is for the young people to decide whether it is easier to criticise others or to see their good points. There is no wrong or right answer as it is personal and up for discussion!

You will need

- nothing!

How to do it

Designate an area as a 'stage'. Explain to the group that the object of the activity is to experience conflict and compliments and then discuss what feels the most comfortable to both give and receive. Try to give an idea of the exercise without giving too much away to avoid the group becoming reserved about what they do.

Set some ground rules with the group:

- Any conversation that takes place ends when the young person comes off stage.

- Any 'argument' started must be abstract and not a continuation of any outside grievance or vendetta!

- Only two people can be on stage at any time and the dialogue only takes place for as long as they want – at any time they can withdraw and the next person has a go.

- If the experience becomes uncomfortable at any time the group stops and reviews what is going on.

These can be added to if the group wish.

Invite two members of the group to begin. Explain that one young person should stand on the 'stage' whilst the next one approaches them and begins an 'argument'. If there is reluctance or uncertainty about doing this demonstrate what you mean by starting off the process with your co-worker. Be sure to make it clear that this should not be too personal. A good example is to begin with something that may be emotive but not too sensitive: 'So why do you support Tottenham Hotspur then? They're rubbish.' You should then carry on until one person has had enough and leaves the 'stage'.

The next young person joins the remaining group member on the stage and begins a new 'argument'. If at any time this looks to be getting too personal – stop!

When everybody has had an opportunity to participate, ask the group to begin the process again, only this time instead of picking an argument with someone they need to compliment or say something positive about them. Once again this will need to be managed carefully.

At the end of the process discuss with the young people how they felt. What was easier: arguing or complimenting? What felt the most comfortable: the giving or receiving of either? Remember to stress that there is no right or wrong here. You may be surprised at the answers!

3.3 Mirror image

This activity works on the assumption that how we see ourselves and how we are seen by others can be very different. You will need to be sensitive to the group dynamics to make sure no one feels uncomfortable or excluded.

Aim

This activity encourages discussion around public image and first impressions and questions the importance of this.

You will need

- two copies of the 'mirror image sheet' for each participant (in two different colours)
- pens.

How to do it

Explain the aim of the session to the group and ask the young people to choose a partner to work with. Hand each person two copies of the mirror image sheet (one of each colour) and a pen.

Now ask them to turn away from their partner and have a brief look at the sheet. Working with their back to their partner ask each person to complete both sheets as outlined below:

Sheet 1:

Tick all the boxes alongside words that you think describe the young person you are working with.

Sheet 2:

Tick all the boxes next to words that you think describes yourself.

Allow about ten minutes for everybody to complete the task, and then ask the young people to turn around and face their partner. Each partner in turn then feeds back what they have ticked and compares this with how their partner sees him or herself. Are these the same? Are characteristics seen in different ways? For example a young person may have ticked 'Assertive' about himself or herself, whereas their partner sees this as 'Aggressive'. Encourage the young people to focus on positive attributes and discuss areas of difference.

Bring the whole group back together and facilitate a discussion around first impressions, drawing on the issues raised through the sheets but not focusing on individuals.

MIRROR IMAGE SHEET

Think about the words below – which ones apply? Put a tick in the appropriate box.

☐ Honest	☐ Assertive	☐ Sporty
☐ Creative	☐ Sarcastic	☐ Funny
☐ Independent	☐ Happy	☐ Outrageous
☐ Dependable	☐ Aggressive	☐ Embarrassing
☐ Loner	☐ Trusting	☐ Tolerant
☐ Controlling	☐ Shy	☐ Sensitive
☐ Spiteful	☐ Tough	☐ Unhappy
☐ Gentle	☐ Outgoing	☐ Loud
☐ Easily led	☐ Greedy	☐ Untruthful
☐ Quiet	☐ Moody	☐ Clever
☐ Cheeky	☐ Lazy	☐ Leader
☐ Stubborn	☐ Worrier	☐ Romantic
☐ Practical	☐ Open	☐ Sympathetic
☐ Jealous	☐ Kind	☐ Generous
☐ Mean	☐ Careful	☐ Secretive
☐ Bossy	☐ Loyal	☐ Trustworthy
☐ Ambitious	☐ Nosy	☐ Mature
☐ Popular	☐ Adventurous	☐ Careless

3.4 I heard…

This is a new take on the old game 'Chinese Whispers'. It effectively shows what happens as a sentence or 'gossip' is passed within a group. You will need more than ten young people for it to work really well.

Aim

The idea is to demonstrate how what is said can be distorted as it is being told from person to person.

You will need

*   nothing – apart from a complicated sentence, which you could think up in advance!

How to do it

Ask the group to form a big circle. Make sure there is a distance between each member so that they will have to lean across to each other to pass on the 'gossip' you are going to start.

When they are ready move towards the young person next to you in the circle and whisper the sentence that you prepared earlier. Try to make this as 'real life' as possible: 'Did you know that…?!' Make sure that it is fairly long and complicated so that the opportunities for it to be misheard are good!

Wait until it has been whispered through the whole group and then ask the last person to repeat what they heard. It should be somewhat different to what you said at the start.

Discuss the differences and then ask the young people to reflect on examples in real life where something that they have said has been misconstrued or not understood. How did that feel? Could they give out the right information easily? Have they ever passed on gossip that turned out to be untrue? What happened?

3.5 If I could choose

This should be done quickly to get open responses and works with any size group. You can change your topic to suit the age and interests of the group.

Aim

To begin to focus the group on the things that are important to them in a friend and promote discussion on positive relationships.

You will need

- nothing!

How to do it

Gather the group together and ask them to form a circle. This means that you can all see each other and should be able to hear what is said.

Explain to the group that the idea of this activity is to start considering what makes a good friend. Ask the young people to think about which soap opera character they would choose to be their friend if they could. Encourage the group to think about the reasons why it would be the person that they have identified and why they think they would make a good friend.

Once everyone has decided, ask them to turn to the person on their right and share their choice. You can change the topic to anything that you think that the group will engage with. Suggestions include 'If I could choose a...

- character in a book I would choose…because…'
- person in a movie I would choose…because…'
- cartoon character I would choose…because…'

Invite the young people to share what they have discussed with the main group. Are there similar suggestions? Are some ideas based only on how the character looks? Is this a good basis for choosing a friend? Pull out the main themes and ideas about what makes a character a 'good friend'. Are these realistic things to want in a relationship? Do the young people consider that they offer these things to their friends? What are the differences?

3.6 Mad, sad, bad or glad

Even if you usually find it hard to engage a group in drama-based games, the name of this activity is so brilliant the young people are bound to be intrigued enough to give it a go!

Aim

To look at how we use body language to communicate how we feel. The exercise is also a good way to raise levels of personal awareness within a group and highlight the impact individuals have on others.

You will need

- chalk.

How to do it

With the chalk, mark four spaces on the ground – MAD, SAD, BAD and GLAD. Make sure that you leave enough space for the young people to stand by a particular 'feeling'.

Explain to the group that each area marked shows a different feeling. You can go on to talk about how in the same situation feelings may differ within a group, and how we often hide our true feelings.

Ask for a volunteer to select the area that most represents how they feel today. If there is reluctance to go first, ask your co-worker to demonstrate.

The rest of the group then gathers round (not too close!), and asks questions about why they have chosen that space. These should be supportive, not accusations or aggressive. For example: 'Are you feeling sad?' or 'Did something happen at school today to make you feel that way?'

The volunteer can tell the group what is wrong – but cannot speak. This means that they have to rely solely on body language to convey their feelings. Make sure that you are sensitive to the group and do not allow anyone to feel that they are being interrogated!

When they have shared all that is comfortable the volunteer leaves the space and another member of the group takes their place. In a small group each member can experience the process. Make sure that you allow time for feedback and review any issues that are raised.

3.7 Helping hand

This session can be done either as a group or one-to-one activity. It is a good start to a project around keeping safe and protective behaviour.

Aim

To encourage the young people to identify people they could talk to if they were worried or concerned about an issue.

You will need

- paper
- pens.

How to do it

Before you start, consider the make-up of your group and how much you know about them. If you have not worked with the group before you will need to be very careful to keep the information discussed depersonalised by referring only to the examples below. If you know the group well you can ask them to think of their own situations. Be careful that you do not encourage the young people to make disclosures unless you have the appropriate support in place. Ask the group to form a circle or to sit so that they can all hear you and contribute.

Choose one of the situations below and read it out to the young people.

'Tom is 15, wears glasses and is the smallest in his year. He hates sports, but is really good at maths and science so tends to stay in at break time in the IT room so he can use the internet. The other kids all laugh and call him 'boffin' and 'goody-goody' and 'teacher's pet' and take his glasses out of his bag and throw them to each other when he leaves school to go home...'

'Cherish is 13 and friends with a big group of girls, most of whom have just started smoking. Because they can't afford cigarettes, several of the girls have been nicking them off parents or asking older kids to get them from the off licence. Cherish does not smoke, but both her mum and step-dad do. Now the others in the group are saying that they won't hang around with her if she does not steal her share of cigarettes...'

Then ask the question 'How do you think Tom/Cherish feels?' and facilitate a discussion around the answers given.

Now ask the group to start to imagine that they are in a similar situation. Explain that they do not have to share what they are thinking, but suggest that they start to identify people that they could tell and ask for help.

Hand out the paper and pens and ask each young person to draw around one of their hands in the centre of their sheet. Explain that the thumb on the hand represents the first person that they would go to if they were in trouble and needed help. Ask them to write down whom they would go to next if the first person wasn't in or would not listen. Carry on until all five fingers have names.

Reflect on the process with the group. Was it easy to identify a support network? Will it change often? What is it about these people that makes them special and different to others?

3.8 Story time

This 'story' is told like a fairy tale, but depicts a scenario that poses questions that are open to interpretation and value judgements. It works with any age and provokes the most discussion in mixed gender groups!

Aim

To open up a discussion around a series of events that highlight love, friendship and betrayal. The story itself is imaginary, but the young people are encouraged to reflect the issues into their own lives and reach conclusions.

You will need

- a copy of the story to read from.

How to do it

Ask the young people to form a circle or gather together in one group so that they can all hear you.

Introduce 'story time', for example using the old 'Are you sitting comfortably? Well, then I'll begin...' routine, but it will depend on your group how you do this.

Encourage the young people to listen carefully for the twists in the story and each character's part in the events. Once you have finished reading, pose the question: 'So, whose fault is it that the Baroness is dead?'

Question observations made and accusations of blame. For example, 'It was her own fault for disobeying her husband!' can be challenged to raise issues around the right of a man to threaten his wife with punishment for disobedience. Explore attitudes – what about the lover? The friend? Who should have offered help? Facilitate a discussion that encompasses some of the points raised. This should also enable the facilitator to identify any further issue-based work.

STORY TIME

Once upon a time, in a place a long way from here, a jealous Baron kissed his wife goodbye as he left her to visit his other castles. 'Do not leave the castle whilst I am gone,' he said. 'If you do I will punish you severely when I return!'

As the hours passed, the young Baroness grew sad and lonely. Finally, she felt so alone that she decided to disobey her husband's orders and leave the castle to visit her lover who lived in the forest nearby.

Now, the castle was situated on an island in a wide, fast-flowing river and there was only one way to reach the mainland. This was to cross the drawbridge that linked the island to the forest at the narrowest part of the river.

The Baroness stood at the edge of the river. 'Surely my husband will not return before dawn?' she thought. 'I will have time to visit my lover and get back before him.' With that she ordered her servants to lower the drawbridge and leave it down until she returned.

Having spent several happy hours with her lover the Baroness returned to the castle only to find that the drawbridge was blocked by a gateman. The gateman was fiercely waving a long cruel knife and shouting, 'Do not attempt to cross this bridge, Baroness, or I will have to kill you – it is the Baron's orders!'

Fearing for her life, the Baroness ran back to her lover and asked him to help her. 'But our relationship is only a romantic one,' he explained. 'I thought you knew that? I will not help!'

The Baroness ran back to the river and, having told her story to the boatman, pleaded for his help.

'I will do it,' said the boatman, 'but only if you can pay my fee of five gold marks.'

'Five gold marks?' exclaimed the Baroness. 'But all my money is in the castle! I can pay you later.'

'Hard luck! No money, no ride,' said the boatman flatly and turned away.

Her fear growing, the Baroness ran crying to her friend and, after explaining her desperate situation, begged for enough money to pay the boatman.

The friend shook her head. 'If you had not disobeyed your husband this would not have happened. I will give you no money!'

With the sun rising behind the island and her last attempt to get help refused, the Baroness returned sadly to the gate, where she was slain by the gateman as she attempted to reach the castle.

3.9 Mirror, mirror

This looks at body language and explores the way signals can be transmitted without words. It works well following the icebreaker 'Feelings' (activity 2.9) that starts the dialogue around how we are seen and how we see ourselves. This can be used as part of an assertiveness project, including bullying and peer pressure.

Aim

To raise young people's awareness of the power of non-verbal communication.

You will need

- nothing!

How to do it

Introduce the idea of body language to the group. Ask the group to consider how they think people see them – as a quiet person? Disco diva? Shy? Sarcastic? Then ask the young people to share this with the people sitting either side of them. Are there any surprises or differences? Conclude by asking the group to think about the signals that they give without talking that add or detract from their self-image. The idea is to explore non-verbal communication further.

Ask the young people to choose a partner to be their 'mirror'. One person should face the other and act out a feeling from the list below. The person being the 'mirror' should try to recreate the body language of the person acting out the feeling and then guess what the feeling is. After a few rounds ask the partners to switch roles so that they both experience being the 'mirror'. You will need to be sensitive to any very shy young people in your group who might find it very difficult to participate. Try to encourage them to work within their comfort zones, but to have a go.

- Confident
- Scared
- Happy
- Interested
- Anxious
- Angry
- Shy
- Depressed
- Bored
- Excited

When everyone has had the opportunity to be the image and the original, stop and review the process.

Is it easy to see how someone feels? How can this work in difficult situations, for example when you are scared but want to appear confident? How important is it to make sure that the messages that people give are the correct ones that show how they feel?

3.10 How assertive are you?

The next two activities can be used together to begin to explore bullying and self-esteem with young people. You can use them with either young men or women, although you may want to alter the questions slightly. However, I have found that it works best with small groups who know each other well enough to be honest.

Aim

This activity looks at the differences between being 'assertive' and 'aggressive' and provokes discussion within the group.

You will need

- enough copies of the 'assertiveness quiz' for all the group
- pens.

How to do it

Hand out a pen and a copy of the quiz to each young person. Explain that you want them to work on their own to begin with, but if you know that some group members will struggle with this suggest pairs.

Introduce the quiz by saying that there a series of situations and possible responses shown on the page. You want the group to look and tick the response that they feel would be closest to their own reaction in a similar circumstance. Most young people are familiar with quizzes such as this in magazines and will need minimum support at this stage.

Once everyone has finished and is happy with their response to each question ask the group to come together.

Read out the questions and the answers and ask the young people to keep a tally of how many 'a', 'b' and 'c's they have ticked as you go through the sheet.

Finally ask the group to count and see which letter they have ticked the most and read aloud the corresponding paragraphs below. They do not need to share their results unless they feel comfortable doing so.

Encourage feedback and ask the young people questions around what they ticked and why to provoke further discussion. Do they agree with the quiz? Is saying 'Please don't do it' really submissive? How could they be generally more assertive and make their feelings known without being aggressive? What are the advantages and disadvantages of each response?

MAINLY A

These reactions are 'submissive'; you don't always need to go along with everyone else! There is nothing wrong with being you and making your feelings and opinions known. You need to look at ways to give clearer messages that reflect what you really want.

MAINLY B

You are comfortable with being 'assertive', whilst remaining sensitive to other people's needs. You expect people to respect who you are and offer respect back. Make sure that you maintain this even when things get difficult!

MAINLY C

Steady there! You will find that people are more ready to listen to your point of view if you give them space and look at other ways to get your message across rather than getting angry and loud. You may be right but no one will listen if you don't calm down!

ASSERTIVENESS QUIZ

Look at the situations and responses below. Some are 'aggressive', some are 'submissive' and some are 'assertive'. Which one sounds most like you?

1. You are standing in a queue for the bus and someone pushes in front of you. Do you:

    (a) Say nothing; they may have a go at you.

    (b) Tap them on the shoulder and politely explain to them where the back of the queue is.

    (c) Shove past them when the bus arrives and stare hard at them if they look like saying something.

2. You are at the hairdressers and she doesn't cut your fringe straight. Do you:

    (c) Refuse to pay and have a loud argument with the stylist; after all, she is supposed to be a professional.

    (a) Manage to get outside before you burst into tears – you're going to have to wear a hat for ages.

    (b) Ask the stylist to check if your fringe is straight as it looks wrong to you – if you are right you will ask her to straighten it.

3. Your best mate wants to go to a club that opens until 3am – your mum says you have to be in at 12.00, but your friend wants to stay all night. Do you:

    (a) Go, although you know you won't enjoy it because you have promised your mum but she is your friend…

    (b) Explain to her that you have given your mum your word, but you will go with her until you need to leave – if she is your friend she will respect your promise too.

    (c) Tell her that no one tells you what to do and get home at 5am; you can handle your mum.

4. You are with a friend who you know has been shoplifting around the town at weekends. Suddenly in the supermarket she suggests you have a go too. You say 'no' but she keeps on pushing you. Do you:

    (c) Shout, 'When I say "no", I mean "no"' and threaten to hit her if she keeps on.

(b) Take her to one side and quietly say, 'When I say "no", I mean "no",' then walk away.

(a) Say 'I'm sorry, I can't do it, please don't be angry with me' – you don't want to lose your friend.

5. You go to the cinema and your date suggests you go see a film that you know you will hate. Do you say:

(a) 'Oh all right, I don't mind going if you want to,' even though you hate action movies and really wanted to see something else.

(b) 'I really don't want to see this film – can't we choose one we both like? You can always see this with your friends another time.'

(c) 'No way am I going in to see that! If you insist you can go on your own!'

6. You are walking down the corridor at school and two people from your class laugh as you go past. Do you:

(c) Turn around, walk back and confront them – who do they think they are laughing at?

(a) Turn around where you are and say, 'Please don't laugh at me like that, I don't like it.'

(b) Walk back to where they are standing to check out if they are laughing at you and then tell them to stop, you've had enough.

7. You buy a top from a shop, but when you get home you notice it has a button missing. Do you:

(a) Ask your mum to take it back – how embarrassing!

(b) Take it back with the receipt the next day and ask for an exchange.

(c) Go back in with all your mates and let rip about the rubbish they are trying to sell – that will teach them!

8. At the youth club all your mates are slagging off one of the CDs being played – it's yours! Do you:

(b) Own up – you don't care, you think it's great.

(a) Laugh along with the rest and hope that the youth worker doesn't hand it back to you whilst they're looking.

(c) Feel really angry and start an argument – who is criticising you now?

3.11 What is bullying?

This can be used with the previous quiz to form part of an ongoing project around self-image and personal esteem.

Aim

This session offers a starting point for young people to discuss different forms of bullying and the effects that it has on both the victim and the bully.

You will need

- two sets of the 'what is bullying? cards'
- contact numbers and leaflets for local support groups.

How to do it

In two groups ask the young people to read the set of cards you are handing out. Explain that both groups will have the same information on their cards.

Ask the young people to assess each of the situations outlined on the cards and as a group agree whether they depict a bullying situation or not. You will need to be sensitive to any young person within the group that you suspect or know has been a victim of bullying.

When the young people have had a chance to discuss the situations and reach agreement, bring everybody together in a large group.

Read out each of the cards and ask the two groups what they decided. Is it the same? Facilitate a discussion over each card – what could the young person have done if they were being bullied? What would they do if it happened to them? Why do they think people become bullies? Discuss protective tactics and strategies for being assertive in bullying situations. Make sure that the young people have information and contact numbers for support around bullying issues.

WHAT IS BULLYING? CARDS

'I have told her before, the reason I shout is so I don't hit her… I can't say fairer than that, can I?'	'Ben says that if I want him to keep quiet about it I have to give him my dinner money all of next week.'
'Miss Betts always picks on me – she knows I don't have the answer but she likes making me cry in front of the class.'	'The boss at my Saturday job keeps putting his arms round me when he shows me how to work the till – it is really revolting.'
'I like football but we have to get off the pitch when the older boys come out.'	'My dad always asks me to do the washing up – never my brother.'
'Orla says that if I want a boyfriend I had better lose some weight and get rid of my spots.'	'My boyfriend says that if I love him I will stay at his house when his parents are away – I am scared.'
'Kelly keeps following me about, I try ignoring her but she won't get the hint.'	'Every time I walk past Mark and his mates they all laugh at me and call me Shorty.'
'If she wants to come out with me she will have to lend me her new top, otherwise she can go on her own.'	'That bus driver always shouts at us when we get on his bus – last night he only let half of us on.'
'Have you seen Daryl in PE? What a sight, we all laugh as he comes into the gym!'	'Like maths? No way! I don't want everyone thinking that I am a boffin.'
'I have tried ignoring them, but they just throw things at my back as I walk into youth club.'	'I like Daniel, but all my friends will laugh if I go out with him.'
'So I told him, Go out with him? No way – he would probably want his mummy to come too!'	'It is hard, every time I come out of school one of them is there waiting for me.'

3.12 Best of friends

Aim

This is an exercise that explores 'what happens next?' and promotes discussion around friendships and the dynamics within a small group.

You will need

- a copy of the 'best of friends scenario'.

How to do it

Ask the young people to gather into a circle and make themselves comfortable – explain you want to tell them a story. If your group is made up predominantly of young men you may want to consider adapting the story and changing the gender.

Depending on how well you know the group you can either read the scenario yourself or ask for a volunteer. Make sure you read slowly enough for everyone to get the 'gist' of the story.

Once you have finished, ask the following questions to provide a framework for a discussion:

1. Who is the 'real' friend here?

2. Who holds the power in the group?

3. What do you think each young woman should do next?

4. How can they resolve the conflict?

Draw the discussion to a close once a strategy for 'what happens next' has been agreed.

BEST OF FRIENDS SCENARIO

Carly attends the youth club every week. Although she has been excluded from school for bullying and is branded a 'trouble maker' by her former teachers, she has been eager to take part in club sessions and is a reliable and popular member of the group. Her best friend is Hannah, who is quieter than her louder friend.

Gemma is friends with both girls. She likes Hannah the best and often wishes that she could see her without Carly, but this doesn't happen. Gemma and Carly have fallen out several times over the past few months and Hannah finds herself caught in the middle, passing messages from one girl to another. On one occasion Gemma and Carly had a fight over something Hannah told Carly that Gemma had said, which later turned out to be untrue.

This evening at youth club Gemma is crying in the toilets and Hannah tells the staff she is worried 'something' is going to happen. Hannah explains that Carly hates Gemma and has threatened to 'give her a slapping'.

Gemma says she does not know why Carly dislikes her so much. Hannah suggests it is because Carly has accused Gemma of 'stealing' boyfriends and 'sleeping around'. Hannah says that Gemma should stand up for herself more and says she will support her if she goes against Carly. Gemma decides that Hannah is right, and storms off in search of Carly to sort it out.

Workers arrive in time to hear Gemma shouting abuse at Carly and Carly repeating her threat to hit Gemma. Carly tells Hannah to stay out of it as she has no argument with her and says she will still be her best friend as long as she ignores Gemma. In the midst of the shouting, screaming and threats of violence Hannah turns away from her two fighting friends and smiles to herself.

3.13 No means no!

This encourages young people to develop strategies to say 'no' effectively in difficult situations. Vary the exercise by changing the issue featured in the scenario. The storyboard can be used in any context.

Aim

To develop assertiveness in saying 'no' to peer pressure to do things the young people are uncomfortable with.

You will need

- a 'no means no! storyboard' for each group
- pens.

How to do it

Read out the situation outlined below to the young people.

Hand out a copy of the storyboard to each member of the group and make a good selection of pens available. Using their storyboard, ask the young people to show what the character could say or do to resolve the situation.

> You are in town with two of your mates. As you walk out of one shop they both start laughing and later show you chocolate and sweets they have stolen. They tell you that it is really easy and very safe as the security cameras don't really work. They decide to make another visit to the shop before you all go home and encourage you to take part this time. You don't want anything to do with it. What should you say and do?

Ask the group to come together and share storyboards. Use this as a basis for a discussion on peer pressure related back to the given scenario.

Encourage the young people to think about the consequences of the characters' actions. How could they say what they think assertively? What could they have done differently? How easy is it to say no to friends? What could be done to resolve any potential conflict between the group in the story?

Any issues highlighted can be used to plan further sessions.

NO MEANS NO! STORYBOARD

Use the storyboard to show what happens next...

3.14 My ideal friend

This encourages young people to think about what qualities they look for in a friend, what makes a person special and how to value friendship.

Aim

To identify the key features that make a trusting friendship.

You will need

- copies of the 'my ideal friend sheet'
- pens.

How to do it

Hand out the 'my ideal friend sheets' and a pen to each member of the group.

Explain that what you want them to do is think about who their ideal friend would be. This can be a real or imagined person but stress that you are asking them to consider personal qualities that they think are vital for a good friendship, not what someone looks like or who is cool to hang out with.

When the young people have had time to think, ask them to list the six attributes that they think are the most important. They can do this in order of importance or not, depending on the group. Ask only that they do this individually at the moment.

Once they have completed the six, ask them to write in the box below the reason why this is a positive attribute and offer an example.

Make sure you allow everyone enough time to think about the task and then ask the group to break into pairs to share ideas. Encourage them to discuss their responses. Are there similarities? Are these realistic things to want in a friend? Are the characteristics that they value in others ones they think describe themselves?

Finally, ask the young people to feed back common themes to develop a group 'ideal friend'.

MY IDEAL FRIEND SHEET

Think carefully and list the six characteristics you would want in your ideal friend.

1.	
2.	
3.	
4.	
5.	
6.	

Now, consider why these attributes are important to you and any examples you can think of when you would want a friend to be like this.

1.	
2.	
3.	
4.	
5.	
6.	

3.15 Without offence

Aim

This offers scenarios for young people to explore around the more difficult bits of friendship and promotes assertive behaviour and the right to challenge friends.

You will need

- the 'without offence scenarios' cut up ready to be handed out.

How to do it

Ask the young people to get into groups of three or four and hand a different scenario to each. You can add to these to make them specific to any issues within the group. The young people then choose someone to read out their card and listen to the hypothetical situation depicted.

The task for the group is to discuss the dilemma and agree how to resolve the situation without offending the friend. Allow 20–30 minutes for the young people to discuss the issues and then ask them to come together again when they have a strategy.

Each group then briefly outlines their scenario and explains how they have decided to sort out the problems. Once each group has spoken, allow time for this to be challenged or new suggestions made. You can always prompt this by asking whether they should worry about offending the 'friend', or questioning whether it is a friendship the two young people have. This can then lead to real-life experiences being discussed if appropriate

WITHOUT OFFENCE SCENARIOS

You are speaking on the phone to your friend. You only have a few credits left and no money till the end of the week. Your friend starts to tell you for the third time what happened last night with her new boyfriend. How are you going to get off the phone without offending her?

Your friend has borrowed your new CD. You have asked for it back twice but he keeps saying that he has forgotten to bring it with him. It is now a week later and you really want it returned now. How are you going to get it back?

You are getting something out of your friend's bag when you notice a packet of cigarettes. Your friend has always said that she doesn't smoke and has been rude to others who do. How are you going to raise the subject without offending her?

Your friend is loudly telling everyone in the group that she does not believe in sex before marriage and that people who do always end up sleeping around and getting a name for themselves. You don't agree at all, but your friend is looking to you for support. What can you do?

Your friend always turns up at youth club with no money. For the last three weeks you have paid for him to get in and bought him a drink. You can't really afford to do this any more as he never offers to pay you back. The club is on tomorrow – how are you going to say something?

3.16 How do I look?

This activity explores stereotypes and is good to use as an opening session for projects around issues such as gender and self-image. It works effectively with groups of up to eight young people.

Aim

The aim of the session is to raise the group's awareness of stereotyping in a non-confrontational way, encouraging them to open up further discussions.

You will need

- copies of the 'how do I look? sheet' cut up
- flipchart paper
- plenty of coloured markers.

How to do it

Hand each young person a slip from the 'how do I look? sheet' and a piece of flipchart paper. Explain that each slip has on it a word that can be used to describe a person.

Ask them to look at the word on the slip and using marker pens draw a picture of how they think that person looks. Stress that they should not tell anybody else what is on the slip at this stage. Emphasise that this is not a drawing competition and that they can use any style that they like.

Give the group ten minutes to do this and then ask them to stop and gather together with their pictures. People then show their picture to the rest of the group who try to guess what the description was.

When all the pictures have been correctly identified, review what has been drawn. Are all the models shown as women? Are all the racists drawn as men? How about bullies and teacher's pets? Encourage the group to discuss how they decided what gender to draw and question if certain attributes or qualities are seen as gender specific.

HOW DO I LOOK? SHEET

Bully	Teacher's pet
Cool	Thief
Racist	Fighter
Greedy	Happy
Sporty	Lonely
Lazy	Rebel
Caring	Shy
Tarty	Loud mouth
Funny	Model
Mean	Gossip

3.17 To be a man

This looks at how gender is constructed in the tabloid press. It was given to me as part of a project with young men, but you could reverse the gender and use it with young women too.

Aim

To look at the pressures placed on young men to conform to social 'norms' and how the media influences these.

You will need

- a good selection of articles about men from the tabloid press
- flipchart paper
- pens.

How to do it

In preparation for the session collect a good range of articles about men. Try to include international copy and local interest stories as well as clippings from magazines such as *GQ* and *Loaded*!

When the young men arrive, hand them two or three articles each. In a circle ask the group to read their articles and to shout out all of the words that are describing men as they see them. Your co-worker can facilitate this if it becomes a shouting competition! You need to record everything onto the flipchart paper so nothing is missed.

When they have finished ask them to put the articles down and read back to them all the words that have been collected. Use this as the basis for a discussion. Start by asking the questions: Is this how men really are? Is this how they see themselves? Their friends? The men they know such as their fathers or brothers? Who is a positive role model in their life and why?

Look at this and compare any conflicting images found, for example the 'New Man' and the 'Laddish' culture.

Review and identify any further work with the group for future sessions.

3.18 Bully court

Before you consider this project you need to be aware of the dynamics within the group you plan to work with. It may not be appropriate for someone who has either been a recent victim of bullying or who already dominates the group.

Aim

To explore the issues around bullying and to look at the different characters' involvement in a given scenario.

You will need.

- a set of the 'bully court cards'

- leaflets and telephone numbers for local support networks for the victims of bullying.

How to do it

This is a role-play activity which divides up the characters to work through the issues highlighted during the 'bully court'. There are no given solutions as the young people will take the role-play where they want to. The facilitator's job is to set the scene, make sure that no one is feeling uncomfortable and that any issues raised are resolved.

Ask the group to form a circle and then read the following, changing the gender to suit your group:

> This bully court has come together to assess this situation and agree whether bullying has taken place or not. The court will then decide what should, if anything, happen to the bully.
>
> It is alleged that two young men kicked another young person on the way home from school. One then ripped up school work, spat and made further threats if this information was shared with teachers or parents. This is not the first time that an incident like this has happened. Money has also been stolen from the young person and food taken with the threat of violence if they argued back.
>
> The young men say that it is not their fault and that the other young person started all the trouble. They claim that the other young person does not like them and is trying to get them in trouble. Neither will comment on the stealing, spitting and threats of violence.

Hand out a card with a character name on to each member of the group. Allow ten minutes for each participant to think about the role that they are to play and how this could fit with the scene outlined by the facilitator.

In the meantime set up the room so that the circle you had becomes a semi-circle with one chair at the front for the 'judge', one for the 'accused' and one for each 'witness' or 'speaker'. The rest of the group will form the jury and make decisions on what happens next based on discussion and consensus. The idea is that this represents a court.

The facilitator then invites each character in turn to step forward and tell their story to the bully court. In role, the young people can then discuss what has been said and decide whether this is a case of bullying or wrongful accusations.

Finally, facilitate a discussion about what should happen to bullies and how victims of bullying can keep themselves safe and be more assertive.

BULLY COURT CARDS

Victim	**Accused**
You have not told anyone what has been happening to you over the last months as you are scared of what might happen.	You are angry because you don't think it is your fault. Lots of people argue – what is all the fuss about?
Accused	**Witness**
You do not think that you should be here at all. Everyone always blames you; it's not fair.	You have seen some things that have made you worried. You do not think that it is right that someone is being picked on.
Teacher	**Witness**
You teach all those involved and have stepped in before.	You know what has happened but you are scared about what will happen to you if you say something.
Judge	**Parent of accused**
Your role is to listen to each person and make sure that you and the jury are clear what is being said.	Your son has never been in trouble before and you don't believe it.
Parent of accused	**Parent of victim**
It is not just at school that your son is difficult. He is angry and aggressive at home too and you have had enough.	You have been getting more and more concerned recently. Your child does not want to go to school, go out, anything.
Jury	**Jury**
Jury	**Jury**
Jury	**Jury**
Jury	**Jury**

3.19 Crests

This team-building activity works well with any age, and is suitable for groups of six or fewer. Because it does not involve writing it is a useful way of encouraging the whole group to take part.

Aim

To produce a 'crest' that is representative of the group, showing individuals as well as shared interests.

You will need

- dough or plasticine

- cutting tools (pastry shapes, blunt knives, etc.)

- rolling pins (or empty plastic drink bottles)

- a stiff piece of card for each group

- cleaning materials (to clear up afterwards!).

How to do it

In preparation for the session arrange tables with six chairs around them. On each table place dough, cutting tools, rolling pins and a piece of stiff card.

As the young people come in, ask them to take a seat at a table. Set a rule that they cannot move the chairs, so if the table is full they must find another seat. This should prevent you ending up with one table of ten and two young people on their own!

Once everyone has a seat explain that the task is for each group to produce a 'crest' that shows the people on their table. It needs to represent characteristics of each individual as well as things that the group has in common. They may want to use the knives to add their names to the 'crest'. Do not be too prescriptive as you want the group to be as creative as possible.

Allow about 30 minutes for the artwork to be completed. It will take longer if you have a lot of groups. Ask the young people to display their crests on the stiff card when they have finished in the centre of the table.

Next allow 'gallery' time so that everyone can view all the crests. This is not a competition but an opportunity to share. In turn each group stands by their crest and answers any questions the rest of the young people may have.

Review the process. Were there any common themes? How easy was it to negotiate things that represented everyone? How were individual attributes chosen?

You can then dry or bake the crests and display them in the club. A variation would be to produce a large crest that represents all of the young people.

3.20 Group fall

You need to do a risk assessment before you try out this one! Make sure you give clear instructions. If the group is too young or does not really understand what you are asking, you could end up with an accident!

Aim

To encourage the young people to appreciate the importance of trust in friendships.

You will need

*   nothing!

How to do it

Ask the young people to form a circle, including yourself and your co-worker. This will need to be fairly close together with enough space to move quickly to complete the task successfully.

Now ask for a volunteer. Be careful here that the first volunteer is not someone universally unpopular within the group or who is very nervous and unlikely to feel comfortable.

Once you have a volunteer invite them to move to the middle of the circle and ask them to close their eyes.

Explain that the idea of the 'Group fall' is to highlight the need for trust within relationships and particularly friendships. What you are going to do is to ask the young person in the middle to 'fall', still with their eyes closed, and as a group you are all going to catch them.

Suggest that if the young people decide to let the volunteer fall, they should consider how they would feel if the same thing happened during their turn.

Review the activity as you go along. How does it feel to have your eyes closed and place your trust in your friends? How does it feel to be responsible for the safety of someone else? What feels more comfortable?

Continue the activity until everybody has experienced both roles.

3.21 Taking risks

This session is a good way of encouraging young people to see the 'bigger picture' for the decisions they make.

Aim

The aim of this session is to encourage young people to make personal assessments of the risks they take when making decisions so that they can begin to make informed choices.

You will need

- a copy of the 'taking risks sheet'
- pens.

How to do it

Begin the session by introducing the idea that most things we do in life have some sort of a risk attached. Suggest that some choices we think long and hard about, but some we make every day and may not even be aware that we are doing it. A good example to offer is that of crossing the road. We make a risk assessment to see if we are likely to be run over before we cross each time, but are probably not aware of the thought process or consider it an 'assessment' as such.

Hand out the sheet and ask the young people to think of risks that they take when out with friends or are likely to take at some time, for example, walking home alone at night, getting drunk at a party, riding a bike at night without lights, etc.

As a whole group, look at the sheets and discuss:

- What are the risks involved?
- What makes it more or less likely that the risk is taken? Be sure to include peer pressure here.
- What are the potential consequences (positive and negative)?
- What could be done to make it a safer activity (including not doing it at all!)?

Agree some principles that can be used to reduce risks and suggest that they try these out when faced with a decision that needs a risk assessment during the next week. You can then discuss this at the next meeting to see what happened.

TAKING RISKS SHEET

A risk I have taken:

A risk I might take:

A risk that I wouldn't take again:

Chapter 4

Living at Home

4.1 My home

Before you start this activity make sure that you are aware of the young people's living arrangements. For example, a child who has recently moved, or is living with foster parents, or who is recently bereaved may find it very difficult to discuss how they feel about home. This does not preclude using this process, but it may be too sensitive to do as a group.

Aim

To support the young people in expressing how they feel about 'home' and their roles and responsibilities within it.

You will need

- nothing!

How to do it

Start the session by explaining that you would like the group to think about a statement that you are going to make. Explain that you would like those people who agree to raise their hands and those that don't to keep their hands down.

'A home is just a place you sleep.'

Once the group has voted, invite the young people to share their opinions. So for example, Sadie could say she agrees because 'it is the people not the place that make a home', but Jack may disagree because he thinks 'a home is somewhere you belong and are safe'.

Ensure that any ground rules around confidentiality are adhered to and make sure that everyone has the opportunity to contribute. Facilitate a discussion that asks for suggestions of ways the young people can contribute towards making their home the way they want it. Consider rights and responsibilities, for example, the right to feel safe and the responsibilities for chores around the home. Finish by agreeing one thing each person can do to make a difference for the next week. This could be something practical like picking up their dirty laundry or something such as not fighting with siblings. Review next time the group meets.

4.2 Family values

This is an opening session that starts to question what young people mean by the concept of 'family'.

Aim

The aim of this activity is to highlight that all families are different shapes and sizes but should be valued equally.

You will need

* a copy of the 'family values sheet'.

How to do it

Explain to the group that you are going to call out a list of statements that you want them to think about and then 'vote' their opinion.

The voting system works like this:

* If they agree with the statement they raise both hands in the air.

* If they disagree they keep both hands by their side.

* If they are not sure or agree in part they raise one hand.

Make sure all the young people can hear you and everyone is clear about how to vote!

After each vote ask the group to look around and challenge each other or ask questions. Make sure that this is done positively and is not an excuse for attacking each other's opinions and values.

Follow up any issues identified in further 'family' sessions.

FAMILY VALUES SHEET

1. A family is not a family without children.

2. A family is a group of people with the same surname.

3. Families are something that everyone has.

4. You have to be related to be a family.

5. Families should do things together.

6. Fathers are the head of the household.

7. A proper family has a mum, a dad and children.

8. To be a family you have to live together.

9. You always love your family.

10. Parents have all the power in families.

11. Children should be allowed to choose who they live with if their parents split up.

12. You only have one mum.

13. Grandparents are important members of a family.

14. Parents always have favourites.

15. You shouldn't have to pay to live with your family.

16. Parents are responsible for what their children do.

4.3 Picture parents

This explores the role of mothers and fathers and how they are shown in the media. If you are working with a large number of young people, ask them to form smaller groups of no more than six for this activity.

Aim

To encourage discussion around how parents are depicted in newspapers and magazines and produce an advert for 'parenthood'.

You will need

- large sheets of paper
- glue
- scissors
- magazines (ones that are likely to show parents and children)
- newspapers
- marker pens.

How to do it

Equip each group with glue, scissors and marker pens. As you hand out the magazines and newspapers explain that you are setting each group the task of using collage to produce an 'advert' that reflects how parents are depicted in the media.

Ask one group to produce an advert for 'fatherhood' and the other to devise one for 'motherhood'. Explain that they can use the markers to add speech bubbles or words.

Allow 20 minutes to half an hour for the groups to complete their collage. Once they have finished ask the young people to clear away the materials and display their advert.

Encourage each group to feed back what they have put together. Facilitate any discussion points raised. Are mothers and fathers shown in the same way? Is parenthood portrayed as a positive or negative thing? How easy was it to find images of fathers? Are mixed heritage families represented? What about parents with disabilities?

Conclude by asking the group to consider if they think that the media's representation is a true reflection of most people's experience of having children. Facilitate a discussion around the answers that the young people give.

4.4 My awards

Aim

To consider important relationships, what makes them so special, and how they inform beliefs and values.

You will need

- paper and pens
- an ornament or statue to use as an award
- film extracts of an award ceremony.

How to do it

Show the clip or clips of an award ceremony that you have chosen. If you can find one that shows an emotional acceptance even better!

Once everyone has watched the film, suggest that at award ceremonies people want to thank everybody who has contributed to their success, from business associates to relatives.

Now, ask the young people to imagine that they have just won an award and will be attending a glittering award ceremony. Who would they want to thank for making a positive contribution to their lives and why? This should be someone that they feel has influenced their beliefs and values as they have grown up and needs to be something that they are happy to share with the group.

Hand out the paper and pens and invite people to write their acceptance speech. This should be short, but include their thanks.

Whilst the group do this, arrange the chairs around a clear space, which will become the stage area. If you have lights or a microphone available you could set this up to make the set even more authentic.

Once everyone has finished, invite the young people into the theatre area you have prepared. Explain that only those on 'stage' will be talking; the rest will form the audience. Encourage someone to go first to read their speech and accept their award from you. Make sure you introduce each person and lead a round of applause as they go onto and leave the stage.

When the last person has spoken, thank everyone for coming and close the award ceremony in true TV presenter style!

Bring the group into a circle and review how it felt to thank people publicly. Facilitate a discussion that explores further the impact family members, both living and historical, have on personal beliefs and values.

4.5 Family portrait

Aim

This activity helps young people make connections between the past, present and future.

You will need

- a photo of each young person
- large sheets of paper
- markers/pens
- glue
- craft materials (sequins, feathers, material scraps, etc.).

How to do it

In advance of the session ask the young people to bring in a photo of themselves.

Ask everyone to turn their paper so that it is landscape and then draw a 'river' across the centre of the page from one side to the other. Once this is done suggest that this is now a 'river of life'. Ask the young people to stick their photo onto the right-hand side of the paper at the end of the river and explain that this represents the present; the here and now.

Now ask them to think about family members going back as many generations as they can. This can include people only known through old photos and the memories of others. These key figures can then be placed onto their river of life, stretching back into the past. Invite them to write or draw pictures to explain a bit about the person they have chosen; for example where they were born, what work they did or any stories they know about them.

Allow about 30 minutes for the rivers to be completed and then invite the group to sit in a circle and share information.

Facilitate a discussion asking the group:

- What is different about their lives to that of their ancestors?
- What traditions or rituals continue?
- What links can they see between the past, their 'heritage', and their own lives?
- What traditions or customs do they think they will take with them into any future family they may have? Why?
- Are there any that they definitely will not want to adhere to in the future? Why?
- What similarities are there in the group? What differences?

Display the pictures as a visual representation of the diversity in the group.

4.6 You're late!

This provides the opportunity for young people to re-write a typical scenario the way they think it should be! Depending on how big your group is you can do a storyboard for as many characters as you like that shows the different perspectives when a young person returns home late – again!

Aim

To encourage young people to think of the consequences of returning home late and the impact this has on different family members.

You will need

- a 'you're late! storyboard' for each group

- pens.

How to do it

Read out the following scenario to the whole group:

'You are coming home after a night out with friends. You are over two hours late, and know you are going to be in big trouble when you do get home. You promised your mum you would be in by 10pm as it is a school night, but you ended up going to a club with a mate. The problem is that as well as being late you also promised not to go to the club as it has a bad reputation and your family don't approve...'

In groups of three or four using the storyboard sheet ask the young people to construct a comic strip that shows what happens next.

Give each group the task of telling the story from a different character's point of view:

- the young person

- the mum or dad

- the young person's friend

- another member of the family.

Encourage the groups to think about the consequences of actions, what they could have done differently and what could be done to resolve the conflict.

YOU'RE LATE! STORYBOARD

Use the storyboard to show what happens next.

4.7 What they think of me

This only really works in very small groups or with individuals. You need to have built a good relationship with the young people as you are asking them to reflect on very personal issues.

Aim

To gain an understanding of how the young person thinks they are perceived by their family and to open up discussions about family life.

You will need

- copies of the 'what they think of me sheet'

- pens.

How to do it

Begin by making sure that the young people you plan to work with are sure about the boundaries of your confidentiality. They need to be clear that there are some things you would need to share with the appropriate agencies which offers them the choice to disclose or not.

Explain that you are asking them to reflect on what they think different members of their family would say about them if asked. Ask them to think about both positive and maybe not so good points. For example, 'My mum thinks that I am a pain because I don't make my bed, but I think she would also say I am a good laugh because she likes my jokes!'

Hand out the sheet and allow about ten minutes for the young people to consider how they think they are seen. Encourage them to reflect on life at home in general and not just to focus on the last row they had or the bits that annoy them most!

Ask them to share what they feel comfortable with. Are there similarities or themes? Are the comments made fair? What could be done towards changing some of the negative points? Are the good parts always recognised enough? How do these thoughts compare with what they would like to be said about them? Close the discussion by asking each member of the group to say something positive about each of the people they have mentioned on their sheet.

WHAT THEY THINK OF ME SHEET

Grandparents think…

Mum thinks…

Dad thinks…

My brother/sister thinks…

Other people important to me think…

I think this because…

4.8 Rules of the house

This exercise works on the basis that wherever you live there are 'rules'. If you live at home your parents usually set these, but renting or flat sharing has its own share of rules that the group may not have considered!

Aim

The main aim of taking part in this session is to enable young people to share experiences and discuss potential areas of conflict. By acknowledging that these may be different depending on where you live and who you live with, the young people can begin to develop strategies to negotiate or accept them.

You will need

- Post-it notes
- pens
- contact numbers for local support groups and social services.

How to do it

Begin the session with a conversation about what 'home' means. Is it just a place to sleep and store your clothes? Does it mean more? Why?

Then hand out the Post-it notes and pens. Ask the group to consider individually the conversation that they have just had and focus on the good and bad parts of living with parents/carers.

When they have thought about it, ask the young people to use three Post-it notes to write:

- the five best things about living at home
- the five worst things about living at home
- five things that they would do differently if they left home.

Once the group has completed the task ask them to stick their notes in three separate piles. They do not have to put their names on them.

Ask for a volunteer from the group to read out the 'best things'. Are there similarities? For example, how many said 'I get my washing done'? Discuss this and encourage group members to enlarge upon what they have said.

Invite another volunteer to go through the same process with the 'worst things'. These are usually the 'rules' of the house as in 'whilst you live under my roof...' and are often the cause of real tension in the home. What are the major areas of conflict? Be sensitive to the fact that you may be asking the group to share experiences they find difficult or painful to talk about. Make sure that you have the numbers of ChildLine, social services or your local youth counselling centre and that you have explained the boundaries of your confidentiality. It is also a good idea to have information about the legalities regarding young people living away from home, including those in the care of the local authority.

Then look at the pile of things that would be done differently. Review in the same way as the other notes, but additionally challenge or question the practicalities involved in achieving the wish list. For example how realistic is it to say 'I would play my music as loud as I want, whenever I want...' Question if this would be possible, unless they are planning to live on an uninhabited desert island!

Invite the group to look again at the wish list and discuss if there is any way that a compromise could be worked towards which would enable them to remove some of the 'worst' things and add to the 'best' list. For example for the young person who gets 'told off' for coming in late at night this could be a type of contract between them and their parent that they will phone if they are going to be late.

Dependent on how much of an issue this is for the group you can work through each of the negative points and see how they could be re-framed to become more acceptable to the young person and their parent.

Agree with the group to each work on one area raised during the session for the next week and suggest that you review how the tactics worked (or didn't!) when you meet again.

4.9 Family snowstorm

To make this really work you need to support the young people to work quickly and to go with their first ideas.

Aim

This process facilitates a brainstorming session around family relationships.

You will need

- Post-it notes
- pens
- a watch.

How to do it

Before the young people arrive clear a space on the wall or cover an area with large sheets of coloured paper. Hand out a wad of Post-it notes and a pen to each person in the group.

Now, set the group the task of quickly thinking what words spring to mind if you say the word 'family'. Then ask them to write the words on the Post-it notes and stick them onto the wall space. Set a time limit to contain the activity and encourage first thoughts only. Ask the group to be as open as they feel comfortable being – including good and bad things!

Agree that no one in the group can move a sticker once it has been placed at this point whether they agree or disagree with what it says. Once all the stickers are in place ask the group to stand back and look at the 'snowstorm' it has created.

Now ask the young people to go up to the wall in turn and start to group the words. So, for example, all the notes that say 'safe' or similar go together as do all the 'rules' and 'arguments'.

Review the wall as a whole group. What are the main issues emerging? Pull out a few of the major groupings and discuss further.

From this you should be able to identify any areas for further sessions.

4.10 Parent power

These examples of parental responsibility are intended as conversation 'starters'. Smaller groups that you know well are more effective because everyone has a better opportunity to contribute and you are more likely to be aware of issues that may be sensitive if raised.

Aim

To offer information to young people that promotes discussion and debate over the roles and responsibilities of parents. (If you are outside of the UK, please refer to the laws of your own country/state).

You will need

- the 'parent power sheet' (which gives you the answers!)
- additional leaflets and contact numbers for those experiencing difficulties at home.

How to do it

In preparation for the session make sure that you have plenty of comfy chairs grouped together to provide a good setting for relaxed conversation. If you have a 'chill out' area in your meeting place use this, or if possible dim the lighting and use candles.

Once the young people are seated begin the session by agreeing some ground rules. These may include:

- no one can enter the group once the discussion has started
- information shared stays within the group (apart from child protection concerns)
- no one speaks over someone else.

Explain the aim of the session and begin to read out one of the statements on the 'parent power sheet'. It does not matter how many you get through or what order you read them out in – it may be best to start with something that you know the group will feel strongly about to start a good debate!

After each statement ask questions to encourage discussion, for example: Do they think this is fair? Who has the right to decide for a young person? Do parents take up these responsibilities? Do parents have more or less power than the group thought? Are they happy for their parents to make decisions for them? Finally, ask the group to consider positive ways that they can help inform their parents and so negotiate decisions that they are happy with.

PARENT POWER SHEET

1. It is your parent's responsibility to make sure you get to school every day.

   True – parents have the main responsibility to ensure that their child is educated. The Education Act 1996 makes it compulsory for young people between the ages of 5 and 16 to go to school, and their parent's duty is to get them there. The only exception to this is if your parents decide to educate you at home and the local authority checks this to make sure it is appropriate. So, if you don't go to school your parents can be taken to court.

2. Up to the age of 18 you are still in the 'custody and care' of your parents and you have to ask their permission to leave home.

   True – but realistically courts are not likely to make anyone over the age of 16 return home if they are able to provide themselves with somewhere to live and are not at risk of harm.

3. At 16 you can marry (with your parents' permission) and lawfully have sex, but your parents have the right to stop you taking part in sex education lessons at school if they want to.

   True – but only the bits that are not part of the National Curriculum. The 1993 Education Act says that all young people must have appropriate sex education in school, but your parents can refuse to let you take part in anything they object to.

4. You can change your name any time you want, although to do it properly you need a 'change of name deed' which a solicitor can help you with.

   False – over 18 you can call yourself what you like with a deed; before then you cannot do it without the agreement of both parents and a deed. If they won't both agree it could go to court for the court to decide.

5. It is illegal for parents to smack their children.

   False – not at the moment! Parents have the right to discipline their children and this can include smacking. It is illegal in some countries though, for example Austria, Sweden and Cyprus.

6. You do not need your parents' consent for medical or dental treatment if you are 16.

   True – if you are 16 or over you do not need your parent's permission to accept or refuse treatment.

7. If you are charged with an offence and go to court your parents have to go with you

   True – if you are under 16, but they only have to go if they are ordered to if you are 16 or 17.

Source – Young Citizen's Passport 1999/2000

4.11 The flatmate from hell

The idea of this activity is to ask the group you are working with what attributes they most fear in a potential flatmate. It works well with young people who are contemplating leaving home or struggling with 'house rules' imposed by parents. It can be used effectively with the following session, which looks at the practicalities of affording your own place.

Aim

The aim of the session is to open up discussion around the pros and potential cons of independent living and flat sharing.

You will need

- markers
- flipchart paper and stands.

How to do it

Set up two flipchart stands. Using a different colour fluorescent pen for each stand draw a rough outline of a human figure. Head one sheet 'desirable' and the other 'undesirable'.

Gather the group together so that everyone can see the flipcharts. Ask the group to nominate two young people to write up responses to the questions that you are going to ask.

First, ask the group to think of all the attributes that would make someone the 'flatmate from hell'. As they call out their ideas a volunteer notes down suggestions. This can range from something like smoking or leaving the toilet seat up through to borrowing clothes without asking or noisily coming home late at night!

Then, do a similar exercise looking at all the personal qualities that would make a person 'ideal' and easy and comfortable to live with. Suggestions for the perfect partner could range from cleaning up their own mess and cleaning the bathroom through to skills like cooking. The session should be fun so encourage the group to be as creative as they like and put everything down.

Once the lists are up and the group has had a chance to consider what everybody has contributed ask them to form a circle. Facilitate a discussion that explores how they see themselves (realistically) on a scale from one flatmate description to the other.

Now ask the group to look at how this might be reflected back at home living with parents and being more like reasonable 'flatmates' rather than 'nightmare teenagers'. Are things that they listed on their flatmate from hell similar to issues that cause arguments at home? What changes could be made, on both sides, to make things less tense? How could compromises be made? Agree strategies and 'action plans' to try out for a week and review with the young people at next week's session.

4.12 The cost of living

This works well with small groups who have already done some work around independent living and leaving home.

Aim

To encourage young people to look at the financial implications of setting up their own home.

You will need

- property pages from local newspapers
- information about local housing taxes from your local housing department or council
- information and figures for benefit entitlements for under 21s.
- information and figures on average wages for under 21s
- leaflets on benefits for young people and any local youth housing project
- calculators
- pens
- copies of the 'cost of living sheet'.

How to do it

Before you begin the session ask the young people to share how much they currently pay their parents/carers to live at home. If this is nothing, ask if they have older siblings who pay or friends who make a contribution.

Facilitate a short discussion that considers how the group feels about paying money to live at home, what they think it pays for and if this is discussed with them in any detail.

Then, working in a circle so everyone can see each other, hand out the property pages that you have collected from your local papers. Ask the young people to look particularly at the flats and single rooms for rent. Encourage the group to look at landlords' requirements, for example a month's rent in advance or a deposit. Do most accept welfare benefits? Is there an age or gender requirement stipulated?

When the group has an idea of the sort of accommodation available for young people, hand out the 'cost of living sheets'. Make the information on local housing taxes available.

Ask the young people independently or in pairs to prepare a budget sheet for a typical month if they left home and rented one of the properties advertised. Encourage them to be as honest as possible about things such as how much they would usually spend on going out and clothes, for example. Stress that a social life is important for most people and that adults would be encouraged to include this too when planning to set up home. Hand out calculators so that they can arrive at a grand total.

When everyone has completed their sheet gather the group back into a circle. Ask for feedback from the process. What are the costs like? Are the totals similar? Is it more or less than what they thought? What is the most expensive part of living away from home?

Finally, hand out information about the benefits that young people are entitled to, and the average wages for under 21s.

In pairs ask the group to look at the total on their sheet and compare this to the average income for a young person. Does it add up? What is the difference? Could they manage?

Review the session and learning outcomes. Agree with the group any further sessions to explore issues that have been raised in more depth.

COST OF LIVING SHEET

Have a look at the grid below and complete the sections based on the information you have and what you currently spend. This should be to cover a typical month. If there are sections you are not sure of make a guess, but put something in each box.

	£
RENT	
LOCAL HOUSING TAXES	
HEATING AND LIGHTING (may be included in rent)	
TELEPHONE	
FOOD AND DRINK	
HOUSEHOLD GOODS (light bulbs, toilet rolls, etc.)	
CLOTHES	
GOING OUT AND RECREATION	
EXTRAS (CDs, presents, toiletries, etc.)	
TOTAL	

4.13 Family map

Aim

The main point to the activity is to acknowledge that all families are different; they come in lots of different shapes and sizes – all are valid.

You will need

- flipchart paper
- pens
- marker pens.

How to do it

Hand out sheets of flipchart paper to each young person and make a good selection of marker pens available.

Explain that what you want the group to do is to draw a family map that shows the people, things and traditions that are important to their family and make it what it is. This should be done individually with an opportunity to share later. If you know that you have a number of young people in the group who have difficulties in writing set the activity as a drawing task for everyone.

Ask the group to think about their family in the broadest sense – not just their parents or siblings but other people that make a contribution to the way their family is. This can include family friends, cousins, step-relations or childminders, grandparents, etc.; in fact anyone who is important to them should be on it! You could demonstrate by making a map of your own family if you think that this will help start the group off. Stress that the drawings can be as simple as stick people – you are not expecting portraits!

Once the people who are important are 'mapped', ask the group to think about traditions and celebrations that are important. These could be religious celebrations, such as Midnight Mass at Christmas, Ramadan, or Diwali, or family rituals, for example Sunday lunch or a weekly visit to grandparents. Once again encourage the young people to think about things that have 'always' happened in their home lives.

Finally, ask the group to mark out important events that happen or have happened, for example a parent's wedding or the birth of a younger sibling or a special family holiday.

Once the maps are complete ask the group to come together. Offer the young people the opportunity to share family maps. If this is not appropriate ask them to share some of the things they have recorded. Are there similarities? What expectations are there from parents/carers to maintain these traditions? In the future, do they think that they will keep these traditions?

Facilitate a discussion about how family expectations change (or don't) as children grow up into young adults. Are these realistic? Look at ways that tension could be reduced or expectations questioned effectively.

4.14 Act out families

Aim

This activity aims to work through a range of family situations in a safe environment. The cards are non-prescriptive so the young people can choose who they represent. It should be played at a fairly fast pace so that everybody has the chance to 'act out' a character.

You will need

- a copy of the set of 'act out families cards'

- information around issues likely to be raised through the session.

How to do it

Start the session by suggesting that non-verbal communication shows others how we are feeling or behaving without any words being spoken. Suggest this is true for all people including parents and families. Ask the young people to consider this and to think about their own body language.

Next, explain that you are going to ask for two volunteers to demonstrate this. Introduce the set of cards and the game by telling the group that one volunteer will 'act out' what is on the card, in any role they choose, e.g. a mother or sister. The other will play the role of a young person returning home and should ask questions to try to guess what is on the card. All questions must be answered in character so, for example, if your card says 'Being angry', you can reply to the question 'How are you?' by shouting, 'What time do you call this?'

If you are met with a shy silence, volunteer yourself to take the first turn. Often this is a great success, especially if you really overact!

A guess can be made at any stage in the process. If it is correct the young person takes a new card and 'acts out' the next role. A new volunteer comes forward to play the young person returning home and tries to guess what they are acting out. If the guess is wrong continue until they get it right. This should be a game that is thought provoking, but good fun. Be aware that some cards may be uncomfortable for the young person who draws them to 'act out' and if necessary be prepared to swap cards. For example, if you are aware that a young person has recently had a huge argument with her father it may be inappropriate to ask her to act out a similar situation.

ACT OUT FAMILIES CARDS

Being ignored	Being listened to	Being lied to	Being a liar
Being scared	Being a bully	Being bullied	Being happy
Being upset	Being proud	Being in love	Being lonely
Being nosy	Being rich	Being poor	Being kind
Being excited	Being bored	Being tired	Being silly
Being angry	Being worried	Being disappointed	Being frustrated

4.15 Timeline

The idea of this exercise is to develop a 'Family Timeline' with the group that shows the progress of a young person through to adulthood. It allows the young people to explore issues and major events in a non-personal way, as the timeline is not exclusive to any one individual. However, you could make it person specific for one-to-one work.

Aim

To encourage the young people to think about important milestones in the life of a family and how this impacts on the different members.

You will need

* flipchart paper taped together to make the timeline for the wall

* marker pens.

How to do it

Before the group arrives prepare the 'timeline' by taping flipchart sheets end-to-end together along a large stretch of wall. Make sure this is set at a height that all members of your group can reach comfortably, including any wheelchair users. With a thick black marker write the words 'Birth' at the start of your timeline and 'Adulthood' at the end. Explain what the aim of the timeline is and what you are trying to produce together.

Invite the young people one at a time to take a pen and write important landmarks in the appropriate place on the timeline. This should include any event or change that has an impact, both positively and negatively, for example starting school or moving house or parents divorcing. Encourage the group to include religious celebrations and rites of passage such as confirmation and bar mitzvah. Also map physical changes such as puberty, starting to shave and the onset of menstruation. As this is not one person's timeline it is fine to include all of these on the one sheet.

Once the timeline is complete encourage the young people to stand back and look at what has been produced. Are there definite stages of development? Are there specific 'markers' towards adulthood within some cultures? Are there gender-specific milestones? How do relationships within families change as children grow to maturity? You might want to debate with the group what age they consider adulthood to be and what defines it.

4.16 Shields

Shields can be used in small group situations for all ages or as part of a one-to-one session. It is a good way of encouraging young people with poor literacy skills to take part as you can decide to make it pictorial only. A variation would be to do the exercise as a collage using pictures from magazines.

Aim

To encourage young people to reflect on the relationships within their family in the past, now and how they would like them to be in the future.

You will need

- flipchart paper
- lots of coloured markers and pens.

How to do it

Give the young people a sheet of paper and ask them to choose some pens to work with. Take a sheet for yourself and draw a large shield shape in the middle. Ask the group to do the same. Explain that this is not a test of how well they draw and that they do not all have to produce the same shaped shield.

Once everyone has a shield ask them to divide it into three equal areas. Once again demonstrate this on yours. Explain that each third will represent a part of their life. One is the past and should show what has happened in their family to date. This includes their relationships with parents, carers and siblings as well as where they live and what they do. The second is the present, showing what is going on now, and the third is the future.

The present should focus on how it is to live at home now that they are young adults. Are the same people close to them? Do they still have childhood pets? Are there new family members to build relationships with? Are the same things important? Ask them to put a star by things and people that appear in both parts.

The future should show their hopes, ambitions and dreams. Ask them where they see themselves in 15 years time. What kind of relationship do they think they will have with their family? Is there an older brother or sister who is a role model for life after leaving home? Do they want to change things? Once again ask the group to star people that are in all three sections.

When everyone has completed their shield bring the group back together and form a circle. Each person then shares the parts they feel comfortable sharing. Draw out similarities and discuss ideas.

You can take this further and look at action plans for achievable goals.

4.17 Two sides

Aim

This drama-based activity is based on the old theory that there are two sides to every story, encouraging young people to work through an issue from two different viewpoints and, it is hoped, reaching a compromise and resolving potential conflict.

You will need

- a set of the 'two sides cards'.

How to do it

Introduce the session and ask the young people to choose a partner to work with. Hand a corresponding card to each couple, asking that they do not share what is written on it. This is important to avoid the tendency to second-guess what is going to be said rather than working through the role-play together.

You can set a time limit on the activity so that the young people feel that there are some boundaries. Twenty minutes is usually enough, but you can agree this with your group.

Ask each pair to go and find a space to work through the situation on their cards. Encourage them to reach a resolution that they can share when the group comes back together.

Once everyone is ready form a circle and share the process. Ask each pair to outline their situation and how they worked with it. Make sure you tell the group that they only need share what they are comfortable with. Facilitate the feedback by asking questions about how it felt to be the parent as well as the child. How easy was it to resolve conflict? How quickly was compromise reached?

TWO SIDES CARDS

1(a)

You want your ears pierced – your mum has said 'no'. How are you going to convince her to change her mind?

1(b)

Your daughter wants her ears pierced – you have said 'no', you had yours done when you were her age and they went septic. You don't want that to happen to your child.

2(a)

You are going to your friend's party. Your dad has said 'yes' but wants you home by 11.30pm. Everyone else is allowed to stay later. What are you going to say?

2(b)

Your son is going to his friend's party. You have no problem with this but you are worried about him walking home late at night – there might be trouble...

3(a)

Your mum wants you to babysit for your little brother – again. You want to go out with your mate. How can you explain?

3(b)

You need to go to work, they are looking to make redundancies and you don't want to give them an excuse for it to be you! You don't like asking for babysitting help again but what else can you do?

4(a)

You have decided to give up eating meat. You think it is really cruel to kill animals but your family laugh and say it is just a 'phase'. How can you make them see how important this is to you?

4(b)

Yesterday you cooked a huge family meal. As you dish it up your daughter announces that she is now a vegetarian! How inconsiderate! Doesn't she know how long it took you to prepare this?

5(a)

You have seen some new trainers that you must have in town. You have asked your mum, but she just said you had to make do with your old ones – why can't she understand?

5(b)

Your son has asked for new trainers. They are far more than you can afford but he just keeps on asking…

4.18 Family feuds

You will need to be sensitive to the fact that some of the young people in the group may have experienced some of the situations discussed in this exploration of family conflict.

Aim

To encourage young people to reflect on what leads to family conflict and breakdown.

You will need

- Post-it notes
- pens.

How to do it

In groups of up to eight young people, explain that this activity aims to explore some of the issues that lead to arguments and break-ups in families. Hand out two Post-it notes and a pen to each member of the group.

Ask the young people to write down one thing that they think causes tensions at home on each paper. Stress that you are not asking the group to share personal experiences and that this does not have to be something that has happened to them. Examples could include disobeying house rules, forgetting to do house chores, running up huge phone bills or disliking a parent's new partner.

Once everyone has finished ask the young people to stick their suggestions in the middle of the circle and encourage them to review what has been written. Ask the young people to rank the issues identified in the order of damage that they think is done to family relationships. Promote discussion around each point raised.

Now review the process. How easy was it to rank the Post-it notes? Were there themes or similarities that aided the process? What about any gender issues? How does religion or culture affect parents' perception of what is OK or not?

Chapter 5

Love, Sex and All That...

5.1 Find someone who...

This activity needs little explanation as it is based on the principles of bingo, which most of the young people will know how to play.

Aim

The aim of this game is to open up discussions and explore values and attitudes around sex and relationships.

You will need

*   'find someone who... sheets'
*   pens
*   prize (optional).

How to do it

Hand out a pen and a sheet to each member of the group.

Explain that their task is to move around the room, talking to each other and asking questions in order to find a name to put next to each 'find someone who...' on the sheet. The only rule is that they can only ask two questions of each person. That should stop people talking only to those they know already and ensure that everyone speaks with each other!

The first person to have a name against everything on the sheet should stop, put a hand in the air and shout 'Ready!' They have won the game and any prize should be presented. If no one has completed the sheet after a set time the game ends and the winner is the person who has the most names on their sheet.

Use some of the points to ask questions about and promote further discussion, for example 'What should schools teach in sex education lessons?' or 'Who can people talk to about relationships?'

FIND SOMEONE WHO... SHEET

Find someone who...

1. Thinks that the age of consent should be lowered.

2. Thinks that sex education in schools is really good.

3. Thinks there is too much sex on television.

4. Finds it easy to talk with their parents about sex and relationships.

5. Knows someone who does not like to talk about sex.

6. Can state the difference between an intimate and platonic relationship.

7. Has learnt something they didn't know about sex from a magazine.

8. Thinks that there should be more education about positive relationships.

9. Can name three contraceptive methods.

5.2 Relationship grid

This can be used successfully in either mixed gender or single-sex groups because the idea is to promote discussion rather than focus on anything too personal.

Aim

This activity encourages young people to think about what constitutes an appropriate relationship by looking at the different types of relationships that we have with people in our lives.

You will need

- a copy of the 'relationship grid' for each member of the group
- pens.

How to do it

Hand out copies of the grid and introduce the session. Ask the group to consider the different types of relationships they have with all the people involved in their lives. Explain the three headings on the relationship grid: 'social', 'friendship' and 'intimate'. Suggest that some relationships may belong in different areas on the grid at different stages in the relationship. For example, a boyfriend may be met socially, become a friend and then later a partner.

Read through the list of potential people that a young person may know or have a relationship with and ask them to categorise them on the grid. Ask that the young people do this individually to begin with, but inform them that you will be asking them to share whatever feels comfortable at the end.

Facilitate a discussion around the different types of relationships we all have, including any disagreements within the group.

- Teacher
- Doctor
- Mother
- Youth worker
- Father
- Cousin
- Uncle

- Babysitter
- Husband
- Girlfriend
- Sister
- Employer
- Sports coach
- Brother

- Milkman
- Priest
- Best mate
- Boyfriend
- Wife
- Social worker
- Friend's parent

- Bus driver
- Stepfather
- Shop assistant
- Foster carer
- Counsellor
- Work mate

RELATIONSHIP GRID

Social	Friendship	Intimate

5.3 Acceptable/unacceptable

Aim

The aim of this activity is to get young people thinking about their own values and those of their peers.

You will need

- an 'acceptable/unacceptable sheet' for each person
- pens.

How to do it

Hand out a sheet to each person. Explain that you want the young people to 'rate' each statement as acceptable or unacceptable behaviour. Stress that there is not always a right or wrong answer; some responses are based on cultural or social acceptance, which may differ within the group.

Once they have completed the sheet review the answers and invite feedback. Is everyone in agreement? Ask the young people to consider what has influenced their beliefs and values, both in the past and now. Facilitate a discussion that explores this and challenges any misconceptions or stereotypes identified through the process.

ACCEPTABLE/UNACCEPTABLE SHEET

	✓	?	✗
Parents discussing their sex life with their children			
Two people having sex the first time they meet			
An elderly couple holding hands as they walk along			
A young couple kissing in public			
A young man hitting his girlfriend because she has cheated on him			
A young man kissing his friend's girlfriend			
A young man telling his friends that he has had sex with his girlfriend			
A young woman slapping her boyfriend during a play fight			
A young man lying about losing his virginity			
A young man crying at a party because he has been dumped			
A lesbian couple holding hands in the cinema			
A couple having sex in a car after dark in a public place			
A young couple having sex at a party whilst drunk			
A gay couple cuddling at a party			
A young woman fighting with another female who is going out with her ex			

5.4 On a scale of...

Aim

The idea of this activity is to get young people thinking about their own values and those of their peers and open up discussion.

You will need

- a set of the 'on a scale of... cards' depicting situations
- a card marked 'acceptable' and a card marked 'unacceptable' in a different colour to the other cards.

How to do it

Hand out the set of situation cards to the group and ask them to read each of the situations offered.

Mark two opposing poles on the floor with the 'acceptable' and 'unacceptable' cards. Explain that what you want the young people to do is to 'rate' the cards as acceptable (i.e. 'normal') or unacceptable (i.e. 'unusual') behaviour. Stress that there is not always a right or wrong answer; many responses are based on cultural or social acceptance, which may differ within the group.

Once they have placed the cards in a line between the poles, ask the group to sit back and look at where they have been positioned.

Is everyone in agreement? Invite the young people to change the position of any card they disagree with, explaining why as they do it. If the group are shy to do this you could start by questioning why a particular card is placed where it is and start the discussions from there.

ON A SCALE OF... CARDS

A young man asking his girlfriend to show him her breasts on web cam	A young couple kissing in public
An elderly couple holding hands as they walk alone	A young woman slapping her boyfriend
A young man hitting his girlfriend	A young man kissing his friend's girlfriend
A man swearing at his girlfriend in public	An ex shouting abuse down the phone
A gay couple cuddling at a party	A lesbian couple holding hands in the cinema
A young man crying in public	A young man telling his friends that he has had sex with his girlfriend
Couples taking explicit photos of each other on their mobile phones	A young woman telling her friends that she has slept with her boyfriend
A couple having sex in a car after dark in a public place	A young man lying about losing his virginity
A couple meeting on the internet	A young woman lying about who she has slept with
A woman hitting a woman	A young couple having unprotected sex at a party whilst drunk

5.5 How safe is safe?

You will need to have built a good relationship with the young people for them to feel comfortable in participating in this activity and be sensitive to the group's age and cultural background. It works well with single-sex groups where the young people may feel more confident in asking questions and discussing issues raised.

Aim

To look at what is meant by 'safe sex' in a confidential and supportive group. Leaflets and information about sexually transmitted infections and contraceptives can support this.

You will need

- small Post-it notes

- pens

- two A4 sheets of paper of a bright colour (approx 8½ x 11")

- sexual health leaflets.

How to do it

On the two coloured sheets of paper write the words 'safe' and 'less safe' and place them about two metres apart on the floor.

Give each member of the group a pen and three Post-it notes. Ask the young people to write on each of their papers a sexual act, without showing anyone else. Explain that this does not just mean penetrative sex, but other things that a couple might do to show physical affection. Stress that you are not asking if they have done what they write down and that nobody will be questioned about their experiences.

As each person completes the task ask him or her to place a paper between the 'safe' and 'less safe' poles. Once this has been done ask the group to consider if they think that all the papers are in the right place. Move on to discuss and agree a final sequence. For example 'kissing' should appear close to 'safe' whereas 'unprotected sex' must appear very close to the 'less safe' area. Move on to discuss how less safe sex can be made safer, including condoms and the option of celibacy or delaying having penetrative sex.

5.6 Back off!

Aim

This session encourages young women to look at situations and make risk assessments. It also provides a framework for keeping safe and looks at ways to be assertive in situations that may not feel comfortable.

You will need

- a copy of the 'back off scenarios', enlarged and cut out
- two sheets of coloured paper, marked 'OK' and 'Back off'
- Blu-Tack.

How to do it

Place the sheet marked 'OK' and the other sheet marked 'Back off' about two metres apart on the ground.

Hand out the situations marked 1–12. Ask the young women to place them between the two sheets of paper where they feel that they should be positioned. Explain the 'OK' is where they feel most comfortable, 'Back off' is unacceptable and any that they are not sure of should go in the middle. If there is any disagreement, ask the young women to comment and discuss.

For those situations that the group feels are unacceptable suggest ways that individuals could make their feelings understood and how to assert themselves. For any placed in the middle encourage discussion until the group can agree.

BACK OFF SCENARIOS

1.	A stranger asks you for directions from his car.
2.	A youth worker asks to meet you outside of youth club hours.
3.	A family friend asks you for a kiss at a family party.
4.	A boy at school/college makes remarks about the size of your breasts.
5.	You are walking home at night alone and think that someone is behind you.
6.	Someone rings your mobile and makes suggestive remarks down the phone.
7.	A workman wolf-whistles at you from a building site.
8.	A girl from school/college shouts insults at you in the street.
9.	An older boy you meet at a club offers to walk you home.
10.	A man touches you on the train.
11.	A male teacher comments how nice you look in a skirt.
12.	You are at a party and a boy starts dancing very close to you and pressing himself against you.

5.7 What happens next?

This can be used as part of a programme around self-esteem and positive personal relationships. Basically, it offers a scenario and asks the question 'what happens next?' to each of the characters.

Aim

To encourage the young people to look at a set of circumstances from different perspectives and to encourage discussion around love, trust and friendship.

You will need

- copies of 'Jodie's story'.

How to do it

Introduce the session by explaining to the group that they will be looking at a scenario involving two young people and their friends. Stress that what you want the group to do is to consider what they think will happen next, and what effect each character's actions will have on each other, themselves and the group.

Split the group into twos or threes and hand them a copy of the scenario to study. If you know that you have a high number of young people who find reading a problem, read the scenario to the whole group before dividing them up. Ask each smaller group to consider the feelings, actions and potential choices for either Jodie or Dean.

Allow about 15 minutes for discussion and then bring the group back together. Ask each group to feed back the main points that they have made and facilitate a discussion around issues raised.

JODIE'S STORY

Jodie is 16 and very shy. She lives with her mum and her stepfather who she hates as she thinks that he is the reason her dad left home.

Jodie is friendly with young people at her youth centre, although she is quiet and tends to like being on her own. She has told the other young women that she really fancies Dean and spends much of her time drawing and decorating hearts with his name and hers entwined.

Dean is slightly older than the rest of the group and well liked by everyone for his good sense of humour and outgoing personality. He used to live in London and still remains in contact with some of his London friends. He often recounts stories of his exciting social life in the city, including a number of ex-girlfriends, and boasts frequently about the number of sexual partners he has had. Dean is enjoying the additional status that Jodie's attention has given him amongst his peers, as Jodie is considered very attractive.

Dean and Jodie finally get together at a party and become boyfriend and girlfriend. During the next few evenings Dean tells his mates every intimate detail of the time he has spent with Jodie. Jodie does not take part in these conversations herself, but does not appear to object to the group knowing about their growing relationship.

Tonight, Jodie is talking enthusiastically with the other young women about how happy she is to be with Dean. She explains that this is the first time that she has found a male she can trust, and that she does not want to lose him.

Upstairs, Dean is sitting on the floor with three other young men. Dean is loudly describing what has taken place with Jodie since they last met. The young men listen closely and make suggestive gestures with their hands. Dean begins loudly telling the young men that he is planning to take up photography, particularly pornographic photographs of Jodie. He says that for a fee he will share these with them and asks for requests of what they would most like to see. Suddenly Jodie opens the door with the group of young women behind her. It is obvious to everyone in the room that all the girls have overheard the conversation.

Jodie pushes past her friends in tears and runs out into the night.

5.8 What did you call me?

This activity is a good prelude to work around young gay and lesbian issues. As with any anti-oppressive practice sessions you will need to be sensitive to the dynamics of the group to ensure that you are not creating a situation that excludes or isolates any member.

Aim

This introduction explores some of the attitudes and prejudice that can be experienced by young gay men and lesbians and provokes discussion around perceptions and reality.

You will need

- flipchart paper
- marker pens
- contact numbers for local and national support/information groups.

How to do it

Gather together the young people into a circle or group where they can see and hear each other and you. Introduce the session and what the aim of the activity is. Ask for two volunteers to 'scribe' and seat them on either side of you with a flipchart sheet and different colour markers.

Next, ask the group to think of all the slang names and expressions that they have heard to describe gay and lesbian people. Stress that you are not asking if they have ever called somebody this, or inviting them to share information about their own sexual orientation. You may want to develop this so that the young people also share who they have heard use the term. For example, 'My dad always calls gay men poofs.' This can be explored later.

Record all the names for gay men on one sheet and lesbian women on the other. You will find that there are far more names and terms of abuse for gay men than for lesbians. Ask the group to consider why they think this is and facilitate a discussion around the findings. Explore common stereotypes, for example 'butch' lesbians and 'camp' gay men. How true are they?

5.9 LGBT life stories warm-up

Aim

This activity highlights the fact that some LGBT (lesbian, gay, bisexual, transgender) young people find it very hard to share personal information when getting to know new people for fear of prejudice or bullying.

You will need

- a sheet of flipchart paper (prepared in advance).

How to do it

Ask the young people to choose a partner, picking someone to work with that they don't know particularly well.

Now set them each a five-minute task to take turns in finding out as much as possible about their partner. They must discover things that can be shared appropriately with the whole group.

Just before they start, tell them that there is a list of things that they are not allowed to talk about. Pull out the flipchart paper you prepared earlier and stick it up with this list on.

Banned subjects:

- people you fancy
- places you go out to
- hobbies
- friends
- the prospect of having a family or children
- films
- TV programmes
- music you like
- books/magazines
- holidays
- clubs you belong to
- your religious beliefs
- your family
- what you did last night.

Call time after ten minutes and go around the group introducing each other and sharing things about each other's lives. Review:

- How easy was that exercise?
- Did anyone cheat?
- What things did people talk about?

- How did it feel to be restricted?

- Did they find out a lot about their partner?

- What is it that makes up a whole person?

Suggest that these subjects tend to be what people talk about as they share information and seek to find common ground. Some LGBT young people feel uncomfortable about sharing honestly with people because they are too scared or feel vulnerable with people they don't know very well. This is especially so if they have not come out yet, or are unwilling to tell their parents and family. This can place enormous emotional pressure on people and lead to lies or concealment. It's easy to keep a secret for a few minutes, but how about keeping one for your whole life?

Invite the young people to consider what they would tell a friend who was struggling to be open about their sexuality. Encourage the group to make suggestions of ways to show support and identify sources of help.

5.10 Drawing conclusions

Aim

To provide young people with the opportunity to explore preconceived ideas and stereotypes about LGBT people.

You will need

- five small sheets of paper headed 'Gay', Lesbian', Bisexual', 'Transgender' or 'Straight'

- flipchart paper and markers.

How to do it

Randomly divide the young people into five smaller groups and give each group a sheet of flipchart paper and some markers. Then hand each group one of the five sheets of paper you prepared earlier.

Explain that each group has been given an identity and that the group task now is to draw a person who looks like or represents that identity. Ask them not to write the actual identity onto their flipchart sheet, but to use pictures that they think are representative. This could include what the person looks like, what they are wearing, etc. They can then write words or sentences around the picture to sum up what they think this person likes doing, what their personality traits are, etc. Be sure to remind everyone that this is a safe space and unless it is entirely inappropriate no one needs to be afraid or worried about suggesting a trait or idea to include in the group's picture.

Allow about 15 minutes for drawing and discussion and then invite each group to present their findings. After each round invite the rest of the group to guess the identity. After all the groups have explained their drawings, lead a group discussion to consider the following:

1. How did the groups decide what each person would look like?

2. Where did the ideas come from about what each of these people looked like? People you know? The media?

3. Do the pictures convey positive or negative images of the identities?

4. Which of the identities do you think was easiest to draw? Hardest? Why?

5. What conclusions if any can you draw from this activity?

5.11 LGBT role models activity

Aim

To promote discussions about positive gay and lesbian role models for young people.

You will need

- 52 A6 (approx 4 x 6") cards (four different colours, 13 of each colour)
- black and red marker pens
- at least 52 pictures of possible role models
- glue.

How to do it

In advance of the session collect a good selection of pictures from the internet or magazines of people that could be considered role models for LGBT young people. At this stage don't worry if they are positive or negative – that is part of the discussion process for young people later. Photocopy the pictures and place in envelopes so that each group of four to six young people has a pack to work with.

Divide the young people into groups and explain that their task is to design a deck of playing cards that depicts LGBT role models. These should be people who inspire or motivate them, including singers, movie stars and sports heroes, but could also include people that young people know personally. Assign each group a suit – Ace, Spades, Hearts and Clubs.

Give each group a pack of pictures to look through and discuss – they can add their own role models or heroes as well if they are not there. Of the pictures, 13 can be chosen to represent the different cards, for example the jack of hearts or the ace of spades. Explain that everyone in the group must agree before a playing card is made by sticking a picture onto one of the A6 cards.

Once each group has finished invite them in turn to share their choices, explaining why they think that this person is a role model for LGBT young people. At the end of the session you should have a deck of playing cards that the young people can use for other activities.

Review the process and facilitate a discussion; for example, what makes someone a gay icon? Can heterosexual people be LGBT role models? What do young people feel about including suggestions for role models that perpetuate stereotypes? How do the group feel about celebrities/sports people who are thought to be gay but are not openly out yet?

ROLE MODEL IDEAS

Peter Tatchell (Australian – politician)	Sir Ian McKellen (British – actor)	Boy George (British – musician)
Elton John (British – musician)	Derren Brown (British – magician/illusionist)	George Michael (British – musician)
Simon Amstell (British – Comedian)	Martina Navratilova (Czech-American – tennis player)	Edwin Morgan (Scottish – National Poet)
Cynthia Nixon (American – actor)	Freddie Mercury (British – musician)	Oscar Wilde (Irish – playwright/poet/author)
Giorgio Armani (Italian – fashion designer)	Paul O'Grady (British – entertainer)	Josephine Baker (American – dancer/singer)
Stephen Fry (British – actor/comedian)	Amy Lamé (American – entertainer)	Tila Tequila (American – model/presenter)
Alan Bennett (British – actor/playwright)	k.d. lang (Canadian – musician)	Michael Stipe (American – musician)
Rock Hudson (American – actor)	Jake Shears (American – musician)	Rosie O'Donnell (American – entertainer)
Graham Norton (Irish – TV presenter)	Andrew Hayden-Smith (British – actor/TV presenter)	Stephen Gately (Irish – singer/songwriter)
Pete Burns (British – musician)	Matt Lucas (British – comedian)	Miriam Margolyes (British – actor)
Dale Winton (British – TV presenter)	Jodie Foster (American – actor)	Drew Barrymore (American – actor)
Debbie Harry (American – singer)	Will Young (British – singer)	Scott Mills (British – DJ)
Andy Warhol (American – artist)	Ellen DeGeneres (American – entertainer)	Sam Fox (British – model/singer)

5.12 Dear Agony Uncle

Aim

This opens up discussions around personal issues in a way that most young people are familiar with in magazines. It gives them the opportunity to play Agony Aunt or Uncle and solve the problems!

You will need

- copies of the 'Dear Agony Uncle... sheet'.

How to do it

Divide the main group into threes or fours. You can do this as a mixed gender activity or you may decide that the young people will get more out of their discussions if they work in single-sex groups.

Hand each small group a 'Dear Agony Uncle... sheet' and ask for a volunteer to read the letter to the other young people in their group. Stress that all characters and situations are fictional and certainly do not relate to anyone in the group. This should stop everyone trying to guess whose 'problem' they are really discussing!

Once the young people have their 'problem' ask them to discuss the situation and suggest some replies. They can either do this verbally or write a response on paper.

When everyone is happy with the 'advice' the group is going to offer, bring the whole group back together to share problems and suggested solutions.

DEAR AGONY UNCLE... SHEET

Dear Agony Uncle,

I am 15 and really like this girl in my class. She is very popular and is always with a crowd of other girls. I know that she has had lots of boyfriends already because my best mate told me. She does smile at me when we see each other in Maths, but apart from that I do not really know what she thinks of me.

I have never asked a girl out before and I really don't want to end up looking stupid. What should I do?

Warren

Dear Agony Uncle,

I am 14 and have been going out with my boyfriend who is 17 for six months. I really like him, but I said I was 16 when we first met and now I am really worried because he wants us to have sex.

I am happy kissing him and messing around, but his parents are due to go away for the weekend soon and he wants me to stay over. Although he says he loves me and that he will take care of things I am really scared I will end up pregnant. I think I am too young to have sex, and my mum will go mad if she finds out.

The problem is he thinks I have done it loads of times and thinks I am going off him as I keep making excuses. Help!

Laura

Dear Agony Uncle,

I am getting really worried about the fact that I don't have a girlfriend. All of my mates talk about girls all the time, but I am not really interested in girls, except as friends. I find it really hard to join in when they talk about who they fancy.

Last week we went to a party and all my mates got off with someone except me. Now they are starting to look at me when I come into the room and I heard one of the girls asking my best mate if I am gay.

I don't know what to do because I don't want all my friends to hate me. What do you think?

Dan

Dear Agony Uncle,

My parents are really strict. They do not like me going out at night and want to choose my friends and who I go out with. They are very religious and expect me to be too.

The problem is that I have met a really nice boy and he has asked me to go to the youth club with him. He is my friend's brother and I met him at her house when we were doing our homework. My family only just allows me to see her, as she is not a Hindu and would be so angry if they knew what I wanted to do.

How can I explain that he is not what they think?

Rani

5.13 Relationship pyramid

The set of cards that you use for this session are non-gender-specific so work with any group. However, if you have a few blank cards you can make some extras that relate to young men or women specifically.

Aim

To encourage discussion and debate about the attributes young people look for in a partner.

You will need

- a set of 'relationship pyramid cards' for each group.

How to do it

Explain to the young people that the aim of the session is to begin to look at what is important for them in the people that they choose to have relationships with. Make sure that you are clear that there are no right or wrong answers for the activity – they are all down to personal priorities. It may also be useful to say that they do not have to have a specific person that they know in mind; it may be their 'ideal' partner or just the things they think they would like to find in a relationship.

Ask the young people to find a space to work together in groups of three or four. Once they are settled you can then ask them if they need to set any ground rules, for example not to share information with the larger group unless individuals are comfortable with this.

Hand out the 'relationship pyramid cards', designating someone within the group who you know is a confident reader to share what is on them with the others.

Now, set the task for each group to agree a 'pyramid' of importance for the cards. They do this by placing the least important attributes to form the base of the pyramid and building up to one card representing what they think is the most important. It should end up with five cards along the bottom row, then four, three, two and finally one at the top. Remind the group that they all have to agree the final pyramid!

If you have a small group you can do this effectively in pairs too. Give out the same explanations, but ask that one partner from each pair sets up the pyramid first and then the other reviews and alters as they see it should be. They also then have to negotiate an agreed pyramid.

Allow about 20 minutes for the pyramids to be agreed. When everyone is happy with their cards, ask the young people to place them on the floor in front of them.

Now, look at the pyramids. Are they all the same? Where difference lies ask the group to share their thinking behind the decision as far as they are comfortable. Facilitate any discussion and encourage the young people to challenge decisions, ensuring that this does not become an opportunity for personal attacks on individual values.

Finally, ask the whole group if they can agree a pyramid of three attributes that they think are the most important for any potential partner. Remember to reinforce that this is not a trick and there are no specific answers!

Review and use to identify ongoing issues for further sessions.

RELATIONSHIP PYRAMID CARDS

Has a good body	Is a good laugh	Has lots of mates
Listens to me	Has a brain	Is good looking
Does not talk behind my back	Someone who I am proud to be with	Is not afraid to show me how they feel
Chooses to spend time with me	Does not show off to friends	Cares what I think
Makes an effort with personal hygiene	Someone I can trust	Someone my friends like

5.14 Top ten attributes

This activity looks to explore some of the myths and stereotypes around what is seen as 'ideal' for both young men and women.

Aim

To offer young people the opportunity to work in single-sex groups to discuss what they think the opposite gender sees as the ideal attributes for a young woman or man. This can then be tested out in the mixed group.

You will need

- flipchart paper
- marker pens.

How to do it

Agree with the young people to work in single-sex groups for this exercise and to come back together to share and compare issues that are raised later.

Ask each group to agree a Top Ten of what they think the opposite sex is looking for in a partner. So young women will be making a list of what they think young men look for in a woman and vice versa. Stress that they will all need to agree any point before it can be written up onto the group sheet. Question points raised and discuss.

Once you have a Top Ten of best points ask the group to come together to look at the sheets. Ask the groups to go through their lists, enlarging on points they have made. Then allow time for each group to be challenged or questioned about what is written; stress that outsiders can challenge but can't change the points agreed within the groups. Support any challenges, reminding the young people that they are not being asked to judge the validity of the points made. Look at the points made; are there mainly physical attributes on the lists, or is there a balance of looks and personalities? Are there similarities between what each group thinks the other values? How true are these? Are there any surprises? Discuss.

Bring the whole group back together and review the process.

5.15 Myth or fact?

Aim

This tests out some well-known assumptions about sex and pregnancy and asks young people to decide if they are 'myth' or 'fact'.

You will need

- the 'myth or fact sheet'
- a 'myth' card and a 'fact' card for each young person taking part
- appropriate leaflets and contact numbers for your local family planning clinic and GUM (genitourinary medicine) clinic.

How to do it

Before the young people arrive prepare for the session by setting up a circle of chairs. Make up two cards for each person using green and red card. Write 'MYTH' on all the red cards and 'FACT' on the green ones.

As the young people come in ask them to choose a place in the circle and hand out a red and green card to each participant explaining what they mean.

Explain that you are going to read out a series of statements and the task is for the young people to decide if they are a 'myth' or a 'fact'. After each statement participants should raise the card that they think corresponds with the answer. Make sure that you point out that it does not matter if the young people don't know all the answers and that you are not asking about personal experiences.

Be prepared to answer questions and discuss each point as it is raised. Encourage discussion and ask the group to think of other myths that they have heard about sex and contraception.

MYTH OR FACT? SHEET

1. You can't get pregnant if you do it standing up.

   Myth – if you have unprotected sex you are at risk of becoming pregnant however you do it!

2. You can get pregnant if you have sex during your period.

   Fact – ovulation can happen at the same time as a period so you can get pregnant.

3. If you go to the toilet straight after sex you won't get pregnant.

   Myth – only recognised methods of contraception protect against unwanted pregnancy. Sperm travels quickly inside the vagina to the womb so the time to take precautions is before intercourse.

4. If the man pulls out before he comes you don't need a condom.

   Myth – you do need a condom if you don't want to run the risk of pregnancy! Sperm can leak out of the penis before a man comes so you could get pregnant.

5. You can get free condoms at the family planning clinic.

   Fact – and you don't have to give your name if you are worried about this.

6. Condoms are a good way to protect against sexually transmitted diseases.

   Fact – condoms are the best protection from STIs.

7. If you use two condoms at once it is safer.

   Myth – it actually makes them less effective! Use extra-strong condoms instead.

8. Having sex under the age of 16 is illegal.

   Fact – the current UK age of consent is 16.

9. You can make a man ill if he has an erection and doesn't come.

   Myth – a man does not have to ejaculate every time he has an erection.

10. It is a good idea to use baby oil with condoms.

    Myth – it is a very bad idea! The baby oil (and any other oil-based product) can damage the condom and cause it to split.

11. The emergency or 'morning after' pill only works the next morning.

    Myth – although often called the morning after pill it can actually work up to 72 hours after sex.

12. Only a doctor can tell you if you are pregnant.

    Myth – shop-bought pregnancy kits are very effective. However, if you think you may be pregnant you should consult your doctor.

13. No one gets pregnant the first time they do it.

    Myth – being a virgin will not prevent pregnancy and plenty of people fall pregnant the first time they have sex! If you decide that you are ready to have sex go to your local GP or sexual health service and discuss the most appropriate form of contraception for you.

5.16 Sex and the media

Aim

This exercise encourages young people to reflect on the power of the media and consider the messages that are given about sex and relationships.

You will need

- marker pens
- four sheets of flipchart paper
- good selection of magazines.

How to do it

To prepare for the exercise look through a wide selection of magazines and find adverts that feature attractive men and women to sell products. This can be anything from cars to food. Cut them out and, if you have access to a laminator, laminate them.

Divide the young people into four groups and give each group a selection of the adverts, some pens and a sheet of flipchart paper to work with. Using a marker, the paper should be divided in four sections and headed:

1. What product or service is advertised?
2. Who is the advert aimed at?
3. How do the models look?
4. Are there any hidden messages?

Allow time for discussion and then invite feedback, particularly focusing on the 'hidden messages'. For example, this product is for couples, all young people are having sex, men have to be strong and tough, only thin women are sexually attractive. Discuss how true these messages are and how representative they are of 'real life' relationships.

5.17 Statements

For this to provoke a lively, interactive debate this session is best planned for small single-sex groups of no more than four. This works well with young people you have already done some sexual health work with as you want them to be as open as possible.

Aim

To spark discussion amongst the group by using statements that express different opinions around moral and social opinions.

You will need

- the statements below.

How to do it

Begin the session by outlining the aim and stressing that the opinions portrayed are to provoke discussion and are not representative of one person's views in particular. Make sure that you are aware of the cultural and religious diversity within the group and are sensitive to any strong feelings any of the statements may raise. Encourage the young people to accept that individuals may have differing opinions and that this is OK.

Select one of the sentences below as the basis of your discussion. Read it to the young people and facilitate their conversation. Challenge or pick up on points raised to move the debate along. Is what is said correct? Is it true? Why? Are there social or cultural factors that need to be considered? Make sure that all the group have the opportunity to speak and no one is excluded. Close the session by reviewing what has been said and identifying any areas the group would like to explore further.

- 'There is only one effective method of contraception and that is to say NO!'

- 'The age of consent should be raised to 18 for everyone.'

- 'Boys want sex, girls want love.'

5.18 Positive relationships

Collage is a fast and fun way of creating a powerful image or message. If you have a large group divide them up so that no more than four young people are working on any one image.

Aim

To look at positive relationships portrayed in the media and begin to question how young people feel who do not fit this profile and where they can find positive role models.

You will need

- newspapers and magazines (make sure there are plenty that are aimed at the teen market)
- scissors
- glue
- markers
- large sheets of paper or card
- Blu-Tack (to stick the collages up with).

How to do it

Working in groups of three or four ask the young people to look through the selection of media images you have collected and produce a collage that represents 'positive relationships'. Hand out glue, scissors and pens. Suggest that the groups may want to add words to their images either by cutting out letters or slogans from the newspaper, or by using a marker pen.

Allow approximately 30 minutes for the young people to collate their pictures and make the collages. As they finish ask them to stick their work up and encourage the young people to look at what other groups have produced. Ask for a spokesperson from each group to explain the main points and answer any questions.

Bring the group together and use the collages as a discussion starting point. Encourage the young people to consider what relationships are promoted in the media. Are couples featured who have physical disabilities? Are gay and lesbian relationships shown? How are single people portrayed – are the images realistic? Ask the group to think where people who do not fit the stereotypes promoted can find positive role models that reflect themselves. Identify ways that individuals can challenge inequalities.

5.19 Share/not share

This session was developed to use with groups of up to 12 young women, but you could change some of the gender-specific cards and use it with young men too.

Aim

This introduces the idea that there are parts of ourselves that we share with different people and bits that we choose to withhold. The aim is for the cards to promote discussion about what is appropriate to share, how we select and how this differs depending on our own 'comfort zones'.

You will need

- three pieces of card headed 'Share with friends', 'Share with partner', 'Keep to self'
- a copy of the 'share/not share cards'.

How to do it

Explain to the young women that this is basically a 'sorting' game. There is no wrong or right because it is up to the individual; suggest that information is shared at different points in relationships, for example you may choose to share things with a friend that you have known some years but not with new acquaintances.

Place the three headings in front of the group in a line from left to right and hand out the 'share/not share cards'.

Once the group is clear about what is being asked of them make the proviso that if there are any differences of opinion as to which heading a card should go under, the card cannot be placed until discussion has taken place and a compromise agreed. This can take some time if there is a major disagreement, but create space for the debate and encourage the group to see this as a valuable part of the session. You can facilitate this process by questioning or challenging decisions and ensuring that everyone in the group is being heard and their opinion taken into account. The game ends when all the cards are sorted.

SHARE/NOT SHARE CARDS

My dad's not my real dad	I hate having my hand held	I have my period
I have a criminal record	My mum hits me	I like to be cuddled
I am a virgin	I think I am ugly	I wish my breasts were bigger
I like having my hair stroked	I wish I was thinner	I am not on the pill
I don't know how to use condoms	I often lie to stay out all night	I am being bullied at school
I often shoplift	I have been chosen for the hockey team	Sometimes I make myself sick after I've eaten
I think I may be pregnant	My teacher told me I am sexy	I'm not always allowed to go out
I have headlice	I want to leave home	I plan to go to university
I don't fancy boys	I am not sure I believe in God	I borrowed something and lost it
I worry that I am too tall	I am not sure what a French kiss is	I have inherited £5000

5.20 Relationship role-play

As with all drama-based sessions this will lead wherever the young people take it. Often this is dependent on how much they relate to the situation described at the start. The scenarios offered are for single-sex small group work, but you can always make up your own to suit the young people you are working with.

Aim

To encourage young people to empathise with a fictional character's circumstance and resolve any issues or conflict.

You will need

- two chairs pushed together.

How to do it

Set the scene by explaining what role-play is and what you are asking the young people to take part in. Contain the whole exercise by setting a time limit for the activity. This will depend on the size of your group and how keen they are on taking part. You can always negotiate more time with the group if they want it.

Place two chairs in front of the group. Explain that this is now the stage and as you sit here you become the character in the scene.

Ask for two volunteers to come forward. Now read either of the following:

'You are sitting on a park bench with your best friend discussing your new boyfriends. She shows you a photo of him with her and you realise that it is the same person you have been seeing...'

'You are sitting on a park bench with your best mate. You thought you saw him kissing your girlfriend as you arrived late at a party last night...'

Show the two young people to the chairs – these become the park bench. Let them pick up the story from there. When they have run out of things to say or three minutes is up, two more young people go forward and carry on the conversation.

Keep going until everyone has had the opportunity to have his or her say. Be sensitive to anyone who feels uncomfortable taking part in the acting. If you know that you have members who will hate it, try to offer them a non-acting role such as timing the actors to make sure no budding thespian tries to hijack the process!

If the group enjoy role-play suggest that they think up another scenario and work through that one too.

5.21 Jealousy bag

This is thought provoking but good fun! You will need to be sensitive to potential emotions that this may raise to the surface. It can be used with up to 15 young people, but is not as effective in small groups.

Aim

To identify and share things that arouse jealousy and provoke discussion.

You will need

- Post-it notes
- pens
- an opaque bag.

How to do it

Ask the group to make a large circle and sit down. Pass around the Post-it notes and a pen to each young person. Ask them to write on their piece of paper one thing that makes them feel jealous. You will need to agree some ground rules as the slips will be shared later, although they will remain anonymous.

If the group seem slow to start make a few suggestions. This could be something like 'seeing my boyfriend looking at other girls' or 'my girlfriend's best friend' or 'girls preferring my mate'. Once everybody has finished, ask them to fold the paper so no one else can see what they have written and place it in the bag as you pass it around.

Collect the bag and shake it so that the papers get mixed up well. Now pass the bag back around the circle in the opposite direction. As each person takes the bag they pull out a slip and read the contents. If they pick out their own they should fold it back up, return for someone else and take another slip.

Leave space for comments or a short discussion after each reading. Are there any duplications or similar themes? Is feeling jealous at some stage a common emotion? Make sure that if identities are guessed the group does not direct their comments directly at the young person. This is a group process not an opportunity to work through issues with individuals. Invite the group to consider ways to cope with feelings of envy and jealousy and point out some of the potentially damaging and negative effects it can have on relationships. Suggest that knowing personal triggers will help them to respond in a more positive and appropriate way in the future.

5.22 How to mend a broken heart

Aim

This activity aims to develop positive strategies and build resilience to cope with relationship break-ups.

You will need

- red or pink poster board
- pencil
- scissors
- tracing paper
- black marker
- heart shape for tracing
- clear plastic zip bags.

Preparation

Trace a large heart onto poster board; you need enough hearts for the young people to work in threes/fours. Cut each heart into a variety of pieces, jigsaw style. They don't have to be the same. Now, cut extra puzzle shapes from the poster board.

Using the black marker, write the positive ways to 'mend a broken heart' from the list onto the puzzle pieces that make up the heart. On the pieces of puzzle that don't fit the heart shape, write the less positive ways to 'mend a broken heart' from the list given.

Finally, mix up the pieces so that each group has a full heart puzzle, plus extra shapes, in a clear plastic zip-style bag.

How to do it

Divide the young people into groups of three or four. Start by suggesting that not all relationships last forever and that breaking up with someone can be upsetting and stressful, even if it is your own choice. Facilitate a short discussion and then hand each group a 'how to mend a broken heart' bag.

Explain that inside the bag are all sorts of ideas for ways to feel better and cope with the distress of breaking up, some positive and some not so positive. Stress that everyone copes differently and that these are just suggestions. The task for each group is to discuss each puzzle piece and then make up the heart shape with the ideas that they think are positive ways to help get over someone and make you feel better. Finally, ask each group to choose which of the ideas they would recommend to a heartbroken friend and why.

Once everyone has completed their puzzle invite each group to present their favourite idea and why they would suggest it to a friend. Then facilitate a group feedback session that considers:

1. What support do people need after a relationship break-up? Does this vary?

2. How could the ideas in the heart help someone feel better short term and long term?

3. Why are some of the ideas less positive? What could be the consequences of carrying out some of them?

4. What other tips would you give someone who is going through a break-up?

Positive ideas:

- Find someone you trust to talk to.

- Spend time doing things you really like.

- Have a hot relaxing bubble bath.

- Listen to music that makes you feel happy.

- Write a poem or lyrics to express your feelings.

- Write a letter to the person you split with expressing your feelings, but *don't* post it.

- Go see a film that you want to see, that they would hate!

- Celebrate being single by inviting all your mates round for a DVD and pizza night.

- Write a list of all the things you didn't like about your ex and read it every time you feel like texting them.

- Get outside and do more sport; make it time to get healthy.

- Eat your favourite ice cream or chocolate (or both!).

- Have a good cry and get your feelings out.

- Play your guitar loudly!

- Sing with your friends to your favourite heartbreak song.

Not so positive ideas:

- Burn everything they ever gave you.

- Text and email them until they agree to take you back.

- Tell everyone you know how badly they have treated you.

- Give everyone the details of your break-up via your social network site.

- Keep ringing their house just so you can hear their voice.

- Go out with their best friend.

- Listen to every song that reminds you of being together.

- Spread untrue gossip and rumours about your ex.

- Cutting them out of every photo of you together.

5.23 Possession vs commitment

Aim

This quiz considers the difference between commitment in a healthy relationship and possessive behaviour.

You will need

- pens

- copies of the quiz sheet.

How to do it

Hand out pens and a copy of the quiz to work on individually. Explain that it is not essential to be in an existing relationship to take part; those who are currently single can either reflect on previous relationships or consider future relationships.

Allow around 15 minutes, depending on the size of the group.

Form a circle or gather the group together so you can talk without shouting the answers. Ask for volunteers to suggest answers and take time to discuss any points raised or answer any questions.

Once the quiz is complete ask the group to count up their scores and go through the answers. Are there any surprises? Facilitate a short discussion to ensure that the young people are clear about the difference between making a commitment to a partner in a relationship and being possessive of that person. Suggest that being in a relationship should not mean dropping all of your own friends and setting conditions on who your partner can and can't see. Encourage the group to consider the destructive nature of possessive behaviour and ask for examples.

Conclude that in positive relationships both partners maintain outside interests and their own individuality, whilst making a commitment to each other.

MAINLY A

You need to watch your possessive tendencies! You have a lot of love and affection to give but make sure your partner feels the same way before you lay your soul bare; remember love isn't about 'owning' someone. Your answers indicate that you long for commitment, but find it hard to trust and accept that couples should have outside interests. Make time for your own friends and make a point of meeting your partner's friends; that way you can enjoy time alone as well as socialising together.

MAINLY B

You may not be ready for a committed relationship quite yet! Your answers indicate that at the moment your priorities are your friends and whilst it is great that you realise how important outside interests are in a healthy relationship, without time spent as a couple it is hard to develop trust and respect. If you do meet someone you really like, try to make space in your life for them and give them the opportunity to get to know you.

MAINLY C

You are committed but not possessive! You are relaxed and up for a laugh and realise that for a relationship to work you both need your own space. It is important to respect each other's privacy and develop trust between you. You understand that just because your partner isn't with you 24/7 it doesn't mean they aren't interested! You also realise how important it is to keep up with friends and maintain your support network regardless of who else is in your life.

A relationship like this has all the necessary ingredients to go vintage!

POSSESSION VS COMMITMENT QUIZ

Do you know the difference?

1. Your ideal partner is…

    (a) Someone who is yours and yours alone.

    (b) Someone who has their own life and doesn't get in your way.

    (c) Someone you can enjoy time alone with, as well as going out together with mutual friends.

2. If you aren't seeing someone you feel…

    (a) Sad and left out – it is really important for you to be in a relationship.

    (b) Great – you are perfectly happy being single.

    (c) Fine – it is nice to have someone special but there are plenty of exciting things to see and do until that happens

3. When you are going out with someone you…

    (a) Spend all of your time together, just the two of you in your own special world.

    (b) Don't change your lifestyle; you can see each other when there is time.

    (c) Enjoy your time together but make sure you still see your friends.

4. If you could choose you'd see your partner…

    (a) Every day and every night.

    (b) Once a week.

    (c) Two or three times a week.

5. You say 'I love you'…

    (a) All the time – and you expect them to do the same.

    (b) Only if they say it first.

    (c) Only when the time is right and you are sure of your feelings.

6. You call to arrange a date and the phone keeps going to voicemail. Do you...

   (a) Leave 20 messages then go round their house to find out what is going on. You refuse to be ignored!

   (b) Forget it; they will probably call later.

   (c) Leave a voicemail telling them you called and will try again later.

7. You are both given free tickets to a gig but you can't go. Do you...

   (a) Insist that neither of you go and demand both tickets to make sure.

   (b) Sell your ticket.

   (c) Feel sad that you will miss sharing the experience, but offer your ticket so someone else can go.

8. Your partner gets a text from an ex. Do you...

   (a) Demand to read it and sulk for days if they refuse.

   (b) Take no notice.

   (c) Ask what it says, but respect their privacy if they don't want to tell you. You trust them.

9. You want to spend Christmas together, but your partner wants to spend it with their family. Do you...

   (a) Demand that they decide who means more; you or them. Christmas is a time for couples and you don't want it ruined.

   (b) Agree to meet after the festive season; Christmas is a time for families.

   (c) Compromise; talk about it to find a way that time can be spent alone and with friends and family.

10. If you split up you would...

   (a) Text, email and call until they took you back; you belong together.

   (b) Find someone else pretty soon – these things happen.

   (c) Take time out to think about what went wrong and try to stay friends.

5.24 Healthy relationships

Aim

This activity helps young people consider what a positive, healthy relationship is and reflect on some of the indicators of a less positive one.

You will need

- sets of the 'relationships cards'

- envelopes to put the cards in

- two extra cards for each pack – 'Being in a healthy relationship' and 'Being in an unhealthy relationship'.

How to do it

Divide the young people up into smaller groups of three or four. As this is a subject that may bring up personal feelings and emotions it is a good idea to discuss the main group contract already in place and add any extra 'rules' that will enable comfortable sharing and discussion.

Hand out the activity packs, one per group. Explain that inside the packs are cards with different statements on them and two cards marked 'Being in a healthy relationship' and 'Being in an unhealthy relationship'. The task is to discuss each of the statements and then decide if they should go onto the 'healthy' or 'unhealthy' relationship pile. If there are any cards that they cannot agree on then put them aside for further discussion later.

Invite each group to offer a point from their 'healthy' pile, encouraging discussion. Then ask for a card from their 'unhealthy' pile, asking them to clarify why they feel it is negative and inviting additional comments from the rest of the groups.

Finally, ask the groups to share any cards that they were uncertain over. Ask the young people to reach a group consensus before moving on to look at strategies to promote healthy relationships.

RELATIONSHIPS CARDS

Accepting that your partner is not perfect	Spending time doing things with friends and family away from each other
One person taking charge and making all the decisions	Telling lies about where you have been or who you have been with
Thinking your partner has 'gone off' you if they want to spend time alone	Pretending to have done more interesting things than you really have
Telling your friends details of your sexual relationship with your partner	Apologising for your partner all the time to your friends
Listening to each other's feelings, hopes and dreams	Being honest about your sexual history and sexual health status with each other
Feeling scared to ask your partner to use a condom	Feeling not as 'good' as your partner
Sending texts all the time as you can't bear to be apart	Getting upset if your partner doesn't do as you tell them

Needing to know where your partner is all the time	Feeling you have to justify yourself all the time
Resolving arguments by talking even when you feel really angry	Feeling 'trapped' but unable to end the relationship
Having sex when you don't really want to	Not seeing your best mate as much because your partner doesn't like them
Respecting and caring for yourself before and during a relationship	Respecting sexual boundaries and the right to say 'no'
Only wanting to have sex if you have drunk alcohol	Trusting that your partner won't talk about you behind your back
Agreeing to non-penetrative safe sex until you both feel ready to take things further	Seeing someone else at the same time as your partner
Shouting, shoving or hitting out during arguments	Giving each other compliments and meaning it
Feeling jealous if your partner talks to someone else	Constantly needing your partner to tell you they love you

Chapter 6

Evaluation and Endings

6.1 Graffiti wall

Aim

This is a good way to review a session around relationships. You can tailor the subject of the 'graffiti' to fit with whatever you have been looking at.

You will need

- a large wall
- flipchart sheets
- marker pens.

How to do it

Cover a large area of wall with flipchart paper and choose a specific theme, for example:

- Why do people get married?
- What is a positive relationship?
- Why do relationships break up?

Write your question along the top of the graffiti sheet to focus the group, hand out pens and invite the young people to write their responses underneath.

Explain that no one has the right to alter or erase someone else's comments – there will be space to challenge at the end. If they see anything they especially agree with ask them to put a tick by the comment or word. Ensure that everybody has a go at expressing themselves and that no one person takes over the wall.

Once the space has been filled ask the group to stand back and review what they have produced. Are there common themes? How many ticks are there? Does anyone want to talk about what they have written or ask about anything put on the wall?

6.2 Word bag

Aim

This review activity uses key words to provoke conversation and debate.

You will need

- a small slip of paper for each group member
- pens
- an opaque bag.

How to do it

Set chairs in a circle and ask the young people to sit down. Give out a pen and slip of paper to each member of the group.

Tell the young people you are going to call out a key word relating to the session they have just participated in. For example, if you have been looking at sexual relationships this could be 'contraception', or if you have been discussing friendships you could choose 'loyalty' or 'trust'. Explain that on their paper you would like them to write one thing they have learnt on this subject from the session and one question that they still have. Explain the slips will be shared later, although they will remain anonymous.

What you are looking for is something that will help you establish the current knowledge and levels of understanding within the group to base future sessions on.

Once everybody has finished, ask them to fold the paper so no one else can see what has been written and place it in the bag as you pass it around.

Collect the bag and shake it so that the papers get mixed up well. Now pass the bag back around the circle in the opposite direction. As each person takes the bag they pull out a slip and read the contents. If they pick out their own they should fold it back up, return it for someone else and pick another.

Leave space for comments or a short discussion after each reading. Are there any duplications or similar themes? Make sure that if identities are guessed the group does not direct their comments directly at the young person. This is a group process, not an opportunity to work through issues with individuals.

You can repeat the process as many times as the young people want to – encourage them to choose their own words.

Close the session by agreeing any additional work identified that the group would like to look at in the future.

6.3 Video diary

This method of evaluation owes much to the success of reality TV!

Aim

To allow each young person space to 'talk' to the camera about the activity/session they have just taken part in.

You will need

- a video camera
- tripod stand for the video camera.

How to do it

Set up a video 'booth' where the young people can sit quietly away from the rest of the group. All you need is a chair facing the camera on the tripod. It looks better for the replay if you have a blank wall behind the chair or a piece of cloth as a backdrop.

Introduce the evaluation process and explain what you are asking the group to do. Make sure you explain who is going to see the video footage and what you are going to use it for. If you want to play it back to the whole group at a later stage, you will need to get agreement from everyone. They need to be clear what is happening so that they can choose what to say! Additionally you may need to get parents' or carers' consent if you plan to show the film to a wider audience.

Invite each young person in turn to enter the booth and speak privately to the camera. This should encourage them to be honest in their responses. This is also a good evaluation method for groups that include young people who are not comfortable reading or writing.

Finally, add your co-workers' and your own comments to the film and you have a complete recording of everyone's account of how the session went!

6.4 Today I...

A quick and easy evaluation method that needs no preparation! It works with any age and size of group.

Aim

To encourage the young people to focus on one positive experience they have had today during the session.

You will need

*   nothing!

How to do it

Ask the young people to form a circle facing each other. In turn ask them to say 'Today I...' followed by something positive that has happened to them during the session they have just taken part in. This can be factual such as 'Today I learnt about parts of the law and how it affects me,' or a response that focuses on feelings such as 'Today I realised that other people feel the same way as I do when they start a new relationship.'

If someone is struggling to think of what to say, offer the option to 'pass' and return to him or her at the end of the circle. Make sure no one feels uncomfortable or pressured into make a lengthy response or talk about feelings that have arisen that they don't want to share with the group.

Close the group by offering a 'Today I...' of your own.

6.5 Circle time

Circles are good ways to end sessions so that everyone can see each other and nobody feels outside the group.

Aim

To get feedback from each member of the group without interruption from the others.

You will need

*   any small object that can be passed around the group.

How to do it

Ask the group to form a circle with the facilitator(s). Show the group the object that you have chosen. This could be something like a pen, but you could choose something with more significance. I have used a small teddy with younger groups or a ball.

Explain that only the person holding the object can speak. When they have finished they pass it on to the next member of the group.

Ask questions that will evaluate the session. For example 'What part of this evening did you enjoy most?' 'Name me one thing you learnt tonight.' Make sure you ask the same question of each person to get an overall picture. The number of questions you ask will depend on the size of the group.

Review the answers after the session with your co-worker and record the findings.

6.6 Wordsearch

This is a good way to get young people to reflect on their experiences, but is not too daunting for anyone who is not confident with writing and spelling.

Aim

To encourage each member of the group to reflect on their experience of the session they have just participated in.

You will need

- a copy of the 'evaluation wordsearch' for each group member
- pens.

How to do it

Hand out copies of the wordsearch and circulate pens. Ask the young people to look at the wordsearch and choose three words contained in the puzzle that sum up how they felt during the session/activity. If you know that you have a high percentage of young people who find reading and writing difficult, suggest that they do it in pairs.

Collect the information and use to evaluate the young people's experience of the session with your own recordings. Any changes or further work can be developed from this.

EVALUATION WORDSEARCH

Look at the words below. Which ones describe best how you felt during the session that you have just taken part in? When you have decided, find them on the puzzle and put a ring around those words.

Interested, Confused, Scared, Informed, Bored, Normal, Lonely, Safe,
Comfortable, Shy, Angry, Trust, Assertive, Confident

C	C	A	S	S	E	R	T	I	V	E	C
A	O	U	P	D	Y	L	E	N	O	L	O
F	N	N	O	E	H	R	X	T	P	I	M
J	F	O	F	E	S	T	S	E	K	T	F
L	I	R	I	U	A	D	E	R	O	B	O
P	D	M	Q	A	S	A	F	E	D	S	R
N	E	A	M	A	L	E	A	S	T	D	T
T	N	L	D	S	T	T	D	T	S	A	A
W	T	S	C	A	R	E	D	E	U	O	B
Y	M	Y	R	G	N	A	U	D	R	Y	L
I	K	O	H	R	S	T	A	A	T	A	E
C	A	L	N	D	E	M	R	O	F	N	I

6.7 Thank you

Aim

This evaluation encourages the young people to think about the role that other group members have played in making the session a success for them.

You will need

- pens
- small Post-it pads.

How to do it

Ask everyone in the group to reflect on the session that they have just participated in. Encourage them to think:

1. Who was important to them?
2. Who enabled them to succeed?
3. Who made them laugh?
4. Who supported them?

When they have thought about it ask them to write a positive comment on a Post-it note and put it onto the back of a group member. Try to facilitate this so that each group member has a note. If you think this may be a problem agree ground rules beforehand so that the group are aware of what is appropriate and what is not.

Review with the group and reflect.

6.8 How I feel now

This evaluation sheet asks for a very personal view of the session that the young person has just participated in. It only works with small groups that have developed trusting relationships with workers.

Aim

To encourage young people to consider the support and help that other members of the group have offered, and the contribution this has made to their personal learning experience.

You will need

- copies of the 'how I feel now sheet'
- pens.

How to do it

Hand out copies of the sheet and ask young people to look and think about the statements it contains. Ask them to reflect on the session they have just experienced and fill in the gaps.

Depending on how well you know the group and the level of confidence the young people have, encourage the group to share their responses. If you do not think that this would be appropriate you can discuss them individually or collect in and review later.

HOW I FEEL NOW SHEET

I am pleased . . . .

is here because . . . .

. . . .

I would like to thank . . . .

because. . . . .

I enjoyed doing . . . .

because. . . . .

I learnt . . . . about myself and

. . . . about others.

I would like to meet with the group again because . . . .

. . . .

My thought for next time is. . . . .

. . . .

6.9 Colour bars

This can be used with any group but has been specifically used with groups with learning disabilities. By asking everyone to use the same process, regardless of ability, you are more likely to get an honest response as the pressure to write is taken away.

Aim

This evaluation tool aims to get direct feedback from the group, measuring participation and enjoyment of a session. Make sure that you ask questions that will give you a performance indicator of how close you are to meeting the aims of the activity.

You will need

- paper
- blue and red coloured pens.

How to do it

Before the session takes place devise a set of questions about the activity you are planning. This could include questions like:

- How much do you think the session is relevant to your life?
- Could you identify with the things talked about?
- Would you like to participate in further sessions on this?

After the young people have participated in the activity or project, hand out a piece of paper and a red and blue pen each. Immediately as you do this explain that the pens have meanings. The red pen is positive and the blue pen will depict negative feelings about what they have been doing.

Then read the questions out one at a time. For each question you are asking, the group are asked to draw a colour bar. This is made up of squares of colour on a scale of one to five. So five red squares in response to a question will mean that they feel really positive about the session and had the best time. Four blue squares and the activity has been a bit of a disaster for them. Basically the more red squares the better; the more blue squares, the more you need to re-think the session for next time!

6.10 Imagine this...

This is another drama-based technique for evaluating how young people feel about the experiences they have just shared. It is suitable for groups of all age and ability.

Aim

To use a visualisation process to enable young people to assess their own feelings and learning.

You will need

- candles and matches (optional)
- music (optional).

How to do it

How you create a relaxed, calm environment is up to you and the area you have to work in. One suggestion is to light candles, dim the lights and play music quietly in the background. I have used New Age tapes of the sea and sea creatures to provide a tranquil setting to encourage the young people to relax.

Once you have 'set the scene' ask the young people to either sit or lie down quietly with their eyes closed. You can use some basic relaxation techniques to focus the group, such as flexing and relaxing limbs and breathing deeply.

As the group begins to 'chill out' ask that they picture a swimming pool on a warm, sunny day in their head. Describe the pool in detail, including a deep end with a diving board and a shallow end with steps out. You can be as creative as you want.

Now, suggest that each person use the image of the swimming pool in their head to represent the session they have just taken part in. Where do they see themselves? Struggling in the deep end? Somewhere in the middle? Watching from the side or desperate to dive in? If visualisation is a new experience for the young people use some of these suggestions to get the group thinking of their own. Encourage the sharing of ideas. Finally, close the session by telling the group to relax and open their eyes gradually as you count to 20.

6.11 Feelings

This is a quick and easy way of finding out how young people feel about the things they have just done. It works with any age, although you need to be sensitive to those with literacy difficulties.

Aim

To get individual feedback from group sessions about how much they enjoyed their time.

You will need

- copies of the 'feelings sheet'
- pens.

How to do it

Give a copy of the 'feelings sheet' and a pen to each young person. Get them to look at the feelings identified and ring those that most reflect how they are feeling at the end of the session. Ask that they do this individually, as it is their feelings that you are interested in. This can be anonymous or named, as they prefer.

Collect in the sheets and use to evaluate the session.

FEELINGS SHEET

Trusting   Naughty   Aggressive

Happy   Selfish   Nervous

Left out   Silly   Tired

Sad   Cheerful

Unhappy   Fired   Frustrated

Lonely   Proud   Confident   Alone

Frightened   Shy   Scared   Loving

Disappointed   Great   Peaceful   Worried

Angry   Safe   Brilliant

Enthusiastic   Included   Trusted

Relieved   Bored   Embarrassed

6.12 Evaluation tree

This is a creative way of evaluating a session, asking the minimum of each young person to create a large visual representation of the group experience.

Aim

To build a 'tree' that describes the learning that has taken place in the session.

You will need

- a large piece of paper with a basic drawing of a tree with no leaves on it
- Blu-Tack
- pieces of paper shaped like leaves
- pens.

How to do it

Unroll your 'tree' and stick it to the wall or floor with Blu-Tack. Introduce it as an evaluation tree.

Hand out a leaf, a pen and a small piece of Blu-Tack to each group member. Ask them to think carefully and write on the leaf one word that describes what they have learnt during the session. You can change what you ask for to correspond with what you are trying to evaluate; for example what did the young people enjoy most? What did they learn?

When they have chosen a word ask the young people to stick their leaf on the evaluation tree.

Review the completed tree with the group and reflect on what has been written.

6.13 Headlines

This is a group evaluation that produces a joint piece of work that depicts the collective experience.

Aim

To produce a newspaper front page that shows the group experience of the project they have just taken part in.

You will need

- newspapers and magazines
- scissors
- glue
- large sheets of paper
- marker pens.

How to do it

Hand out paper, glue, scissors and markers to each group of four to six young people. Make available a good selection of magazines and newspapers.

Explain to the groups that the task is to create a newspaper front page of their own that shows what has been learnt/experienced during the project they have been working on.

Suggest that the young people use both marker pens and cut-out letters from the newspapers to make the 'headlines' and then devise their copy to go with it. This should include how they feel, what they liked best and anything the groups would like followed up in a further session.

Once the front pages are complete, display them on the wall and invite the young people to review each other's, asking questions or explaining sections as they go along. You can then leave it up as a record of the event for other club members to see.

6.14 Treasured comments

Aim

The aim of this review is for young people to experience giving and receiving positive comments by creating 'treasure boxes'.

You will need

- an envelope per person with a copy of a 'treasure chest' picture stuck onto it
- coloured paper cut into strips to fit into the envelopes
- pens.

How to do it

Give each member of the group a 'treasure chest' and ask them to write their name on it. Explain that this treasure chest will contain all sorts of positive messages to them by the end of the activity.

Next, provide each young person with enough brightly coloured paper strips to write a message to each member of the group. Encourage everyone to spend time thinking of something positive to say about each other. They should then write that positive message onto one of the coloured strips.

When everyone has finished writing their comments, they should walk around and put their messages in one another's envelopes. At the end of the activity, each young person will have a 'treasured comments chest' to read on their own.

Useful websites

These organisations offer information for those working with young people and can be useful for updating legislation and knowledge. The author can take no responsibility for the contents, and the views expressed by the organisations included are not necessarily shared or endorsed.

www.advocatesforyouth.org
Advocates for Youth champions efforts that help young people make informed and responsible decisions about their reproductive and sexual health.

www.anti-bullyingalliance.org.uk
The Anti-Bullying Alliance brings together over 60 organisations onto one website with the aim of reducing bullying.

www.brook.org.uk
Brook provides free, confidential sex advice and contraception to young people.

www.bullying.co.uk
The Bullying UK website provides help and advice on bullying issues and resource ideas.

www.condomessentialwear.co.uk
This website gives information about contraception and STIs and offers a free, confidential helpline.

www.cyh.com
The Children, Youth and Women's Health Service (CYWHS) promotes the health, well-being and development of children, young people and families across South Australia.

www.drugscope.org.uk

DrugScope is a UK charity providing up-to-date information on drug issues.

www.fpa.org.uk

The Family Planning Association offers information including a guide to contraception and sexual health.

www.headspace.org.au

Headspace provides mental and health well-being support, information and services to young people and their families across Australia.

www.likeitis.org.uk

The Likeitis website has both an Australian and UK portal. The site offers comprehensive information about sexual health issues.

www.nya.org.uk

UK National Youth Agency website. The NYA works in partnership with a wide range of public, private and voluntary sector organisations to support and improve services for young people.

www.queeryouth.org.uk

The Queer Youth Network was founded by a collection of local gay youth groups that came together to form a regional network supporting the needs of local LGBT (lesbian, gay, bisexual and transgender) young people. It also has a linked site in Australia.

www.talktofrank.com

The FRANK website offers drugs information and support.

www.ymca.int

The YMCA (Young Men's Christian Association) is a world-wide ecumenical Christian voluntary movement for women and men with special emphasis on, and the genuine involvement of, young people. This site has links to UK, US and Australian sites.

www.ywca.org

The YWCA (Young Women's Christian Association) is the oldest and largest multicultural women's association in the world.